AUTOMOBILE ARCHAEOLOGY

David Burgess-Wise

Foreword by Robert A. Lutz
Chairman, Ford of Europe

 Patrick Stephens, Cambridge

Title pages *Enamelled signs of all kinds are visible in this photograph of a London Napier agency circa 1913, taken from a glass negative found in Wales in 1979.*

First published 1981

British Library Cataloguing in Publication Data

Burgess-Wise, David
  Automobile archaeology.
  1. Automobiles—History
  I.Title
  629.22'22'0904   TL15

  ISBN 0 85059 455 3

Text photoset in 10 on 11 pt English Times by Manuset Limited, Baldock, Herts. Printed in Great Britain on 100 gsm matt coated cartridge by St Edmundsbury Press, Bury St Edmunds, Suffolk, and bound by Weatherby Woolnough, Wellingborough, Northants, for the publishers Patrick Stephens Limited, Bar Hill, Cambridge, CB3 8EL, England.

Contents

Foreword

Robert A. Lutz, Chairman, Ford of Europe

It is trite to say that the automobile has changed society, and yet few of us ever stop to think that this product of human technical genius, fascinating in itself, has had an even more profound effect on our geography, our demographic patterns, our employment, and even on our art, our culture, our leisure and our behaviour. We live in a world which, shaped by the automobile, is now, in turn, shaping the car as well as the men who build it. And throughout the course of past and future history of the automobile there will be places, events, marques and men worthy of being researched and chronicled.

This then is an automotive book which does not focus primarily on the automobile itself. Rather, it provides the reader with a fascinating amount of well-researched information on the men who shaped the automobile business, the institutions that sprang from it, as well as the automotive-related places and products which have so tightly interwoven the motor car into the fabric of our lives. Archaeologists of the dim future will marvel, as they dig out well-preserved artefacts, at the all pervasiveness of the automobile in the life of 20th century man.

Introduction

Early motorcars have fascinated me as long as I can remember; one of my earliest memories is of the polished aluminium Austin Seven tourer my uncle owned during the war, a car which seemed infinitely big and glamorous to my three-year-old eyes (I never forgave him for trading it in for a Model Y Ford saloon shortly after VE Day). So it was natural that when I acquired independent mobility in my mid teens that I began hunting early cars, which at that time—the mid-1950s—could be found parked (or abandoned) on almost every street corner. Vehicles of the most astounding rarity were still in everyday use; during the Suez Crisis I managed to get to school most days by thumbing lifts from vintage cars only and when I bought my 1927 Clyno in 1961 it was being used daily by two students who were commuting into central London.

Along with hunting down the cars, I also began to collect the literature of early motoring, aided by fortuitous finds such as a pile of early catalogues baled up ready for the wastepaper man. Visits to breakers' yards, often in a friend's 1926 Bullnose Morris-Cowley, were also part of my motoring scene. In those days breakers 'were places of romance, with veteran and vintage cars abounding rather than the great heaps of discarded pressed steel boxes, as soulless as old refrigerators, which feature in modern breakers'.

In the past quarter-century, I have travelled thousands of miles in quest of various aspects of motoring history and in this book I have tried to set down some of the discoveries I have made on those journeys in the hope that it may start others on similar quests. For the motor vehicle has been the most significant social influence in the shaping of our modern world and its history deserves to be recorded with the same degree of attention that is paid to unearthing relics of ancient civilisations.

Motoring has touched many aspects of everyday life, and in this book I have indicated those which are likely to be of interest to would-be motoring historians in the hope that they may obtain as much pleasure from the pursuit of motoring past as I have had. For the chase has been a rewarding one, with discoveries of pure serendipity which have illuminated many previously dark corners of history. It has taken me across Western Europe, and if there is a bias towards France in some areas of this book, it is because France was the cradle of motoring, and still abounds in monuments and motor cars which cannot be equalled elsewhere in the world. Indeed, only a couple of weeks ago I heard of a 1902 Paris-Vienna Renault racing car stored in a shed near Paris. The survival of such vehicles is all the more remarkable when one considers the *loi scelerat* enforced during the German occupation of France, when pre 1925 cars were compulsorily broken for scrap. Mind you, France cannot boast Europe's biggest car collection, despite the magpie antics of the now-legendary brothers Schlumpf. That honour belongs to Ghislain Mahy, of Ghent in Belgium, who owns over 700 vehicles and, at the age of 73 at the time of writing, was still working 12 hours a day, six days a week, on the restoration of his cars.

Many people have helped, directly or indirectly, with this book; special thanks for material provided go to Michelin, Ford Archives in the United States and Ford of Britain's Photographic Department, and Daimler-Benz in Germany. Jacques Potherat in France helped me discover 'La Ville Lumière's' ancient car plants, while in England Paul Foulkes-Halbard willingly gave me access to his unique collection of automobiliana. Thanks, too, to Gottlieb, Carl, Henry, Amédée and all those other pioneers without whom the motor car would never have become reality.

The author's 1927 Clyno 10.8 hp Royal Tourer, a typical vintage light car, was originally owned by Blackpool's biggest fruit and vegetable merchant.

1 The Sites

Origins

One of the beauties of researching the origins of the automobile is that you can actually see where it all started. In the summer of 1979 I drove into the little town of Void in Lorraine on the eastern borders of France. Here, almost 250 years before in 1725, Nicholas Joseph Cugnot was born, In 1769, to the order of the French Minister of War, he began work on a steam powered artillery tractor, known as a *fardier*, which made a number of inconclusive runs in 1770. To celebrate Cugnot's achievement in building the first recorded man-carrying self-propelled vehicle, a monument was erected in his home town. It stands today in a little square next to the gendarmerie, with traffic roaring behind it on a new bypass road. Cugnot can hardly have imagined the change that the horseless carriage has wrought in the everyday life of the world. Certainly Void must be a very different town today from what it was when Cugnot was born there in 1729. And one can still see Cugnot's *fardier* today, in the Conservatoire des Arts et Métiers in Paris. Having been locked away after a collision with a wall so that it would cause no further damage, it had remained in store until after the French Revolution. Napoleon heard of the machine and had it put back into running order, but his tests also proved abortive. So it was once again put back in the Conservatoire and is there to this day.

The Conservatoire des Arts et Métiers, the equivalent of the British Science Museum, has its transport section housed in the nave of an old church. Here there is a remarkable collection of early vehicles, of which the undoubted prize is the Cugnot. But there are also many other historic vehicles, including the 1873 Bollée steam carriage *L'Obéissante*, the first successful road steamer built by Amédée Bollée *père*, the descendant of a long line of bell-founders from Le Mans, who was fascinated with the concept of a self-propelled vehicle. His ambitious ideas never achieved their full realisation, but technically his inventions were well ahead of their time. *L'Obéissante*, for example, has independent suspension all round, geometrically correct steering and two V-twin steam engines, each one driving a separate rear wheel to give both a differential action and the ability to tighten up the vehicle's turning circle by providing more power to one wheel than to the other. And, of course, having two separate engines was also a useful get-you-home insurance. *L'Obéissante* made perhaps the first long distance motor tour, from Le Mans to Paris, breaking a claimed 95 traffic regulations *en route*.

The Conservatoire also has one of the gas engines developed by Jean-Joseph

Left *In 1969, exactly 200 years after Cugnot's first carriage was built, this obelisk was erected on the surviving base of the Void monument by French and German automobile clubs.*

Below *The base of the Cugnot memorial carries a bas-relief of the 1770* fardier.

Etienne Lenoir, constructor of the world's first recorded internal combustion car. Lenoir's vehicle, of which there is also a model in the Conservatoire, was said to have made the journey from Paris to Vincennes several times, though its progress was punctuated by frequent breakdowns before 1863, when Lenoir sold it to the Czar of Russia and despatched it to St Petersburg. Documents recording the sale came to light in 1905 but, although a search was made of the Imperial stables, no trace was found of the vehicle. Perhaps it still exists in some Leningrad lock-up, a trophy for an enterprising automobile archaeologist.

The first motor museums

Progress in the early days of motoring was so rapid that as early as 1903 the Honourable C.S. Rolls was displaying a Panhard which had run in the 1896 Paris-Marseilles Race as 'a relic of the past'. Not long after that, that famous pioneer motorist, Montague Grahame-White, was driving to Marseilles in a 90 hp Mercedes owned by James Gordon Bennett when he stopped at a café on the outskirts of Toulon run by a retired P & O captain named Tom Turner, brother of Rowley Turner who had brought the first cycle to Coventry in 1868. Tom Turner had invested his life savings in the café which had a two acre property attached: on this land stood a chapel, once used by local fishermen, which he had converted into a workshop and garage for his collection of early motor-cycles and cars. These included a twin-cylinder horizontal-engined air-cooled Léon Bollée, claimed to be one of only three built in 1898 and the tubular-framed Gobron Brillié 120 hp racing car specially built for the American sportsman, Burton, to compete in the Coupe de l'Esterel in 1904. Though the car had covered a kilometre at a speed of 94.3 mph, it was unreliable, as 'excessive elimination of weight without due regard to strength brought out the failure of an extremely fast competitor in racing events'. Turner also had a collection of early pedal cycles and car engines, the latter including an 1895 4½ hp Panhard engine which had been sectioned to reveal its working parts.

Others, it seems, were not interested in acquiring early cars: there was a curious tombola at the 1902 Paris Salon in which the first prize was an 1896 Panhard, with a second prize a De Dion voiturette 'not of the newest vintage'. Thereafter the prizes 'fell by easy stages through fur motoring coats etc to a tyre pump'. Though the tombola apparently contributed to the record attendance at the show, no one came forward to claim either of the cars. After 48 hours had elapsed, they were auctioned for charity, and *The Autocar* wondered whether 'some unconscious English visitors, unable to read French, had won these valuable prizes'.

The first public exhibition of early motor cars took place at the 1907 Paris Salon. As this was the tenth International Automobile Exposition organised by the Automobile Club of France in Paris, the organisers of the Salon mounted a retrospective exhibition of historic vehicles. They also noted that of all the exhibitors at the Salon that year only ten had shown at every Salon since 1897. These were: De Diétrich, De Dion Bouton, Delahaye, Decauville, Compagnie Française des Voitures Automobile, Kriéger, Mors, Panhard & Levassor, Peugeot and Rochet Schneider. Some of the vehicles which the Salon's organisers brought together have survived in French museums; but never before or since had such an outstanding collection of historic vehicles been gathered under one roof, in this case the Invalides annexe to the Grand Palais

Exhibition Hall. The list of exhibits is worth repeating for it includes virtually every significant vehicle produced during the formative years of the French motor industry, at a time when it led the world:

1770 — Cugnot Steam Carriage (belonging to the Conservatoire des Arts et Métiers)
1878 — Steam carriage La Mancelle (belonging to M Amédée Bollée, *père*)
1885 — Steam tricycle (belonging to De Dion Bouton)
1886 — Steam carriage (belonging to De Dion Bouton)
1887 — Motorcycle (belonging to the Daimler Company); first experimental Serpollet engine (belonging to MM Jolly)
1889 — Serpollet steam car (belonging to M Letoile)
1890 — Steam carriage (belonging to MM Suet frères)
1891 — Serpollet car (belonging to M Collette)
1892 — Panhard & Levassor (belonging to M Martineau); Panhard & Levassor car (belonging to L'Auto-Palace); Daimler car (belonging to the Daimler Co)
1893 — Steam drag (belonging to the De Dion Bouton Company); Barras Steam Tricycle (belonging to Dr Bommaer)
1895 — Peugeot Paris-Bordeaux-Paris car (belonging to les Fils de Peugeot frères); Jenatzy electric car, built by the Compagnie Internationale des Transports Automobiles (belonging to M Gimé); Daimler car (belonging to the Daimler Co)
1896 — Electric carriage (belonging to M Darracq); Panhard & Levassor Cab (belonging to M Deutsch de la Meurthe)
1897 — Delahaye (belonging to Dr Nitot); Landry et Beyroux car (belonging to Madame Barbereau-Bergeon); Fouillaron voiturette (belonging to M Fafiotte); Berliet car (belonging to M Berliet); Troïka car, built on Daniel Augé's system (belonging to MM Niclausse); Panhard & Levassor car (belonging to Dr Darsonval); Delahaye voiturette (belonging to the Duchess d'Uzès)

1898 — First Renault voiturette (belonging to Renault frères); Monnart
Electric Carriage (belonging to M Cottenet); Jeantaud electric car
(belonging to Michelin); Amédée Bollée Car (belonging to Count
Bertier de Sauvigny); Hurtu car (belonging to Madame Raimond);
Electric car *La Jamais Contente* (belonging to M Jenatzy); first Bardon
car (belonging to M Bardon)

1898 — Gobron Brillié car (belonging to M Chevalier); Vallée racing car
La Pantoufle (belonging to Dr Lehwess)

1900 — Petit Coupé Renault (belonging to M Raffard); De Diétrich (belonging
to Baron de Turckheim); Berliet car (belonging to M Berliet); Georges
Richard car (belonging to M Georges Richard)

1901 — Renault Paris-Bordeaux car (belonging to M Baliman); Renault Paris-
Berlin car (belonging to M Coucurte); Mors Paris-Berlin car
(belonging to Mors)

1902 — Darracq Paris-Vienna car (belonging to M Darracq)

1903 — Mors Paris-Madrid car (belonging to Mors)

1904 — Brasier Gordon Bennett Cup car (belonging to M de Gosselin)

1905 — Brasier Gordon Bennett Cup car (belonging to Count Soldatencow)

The next step towards the establishment of an old car museum came in April
1909 when Colonel H.C.L. Holden, the designer of Brooklands, wrote to the
motoring press seeking eligible vehicles for 'an Exhibit of Historical Motorcars
which were constructed prior to the end of 1903'. These were to be displayed at
the Imperial International Exhibition which was to be opened in the middle of
May at the Great White City, at Shepherds Bush, London. The display was to
remain open until the end of October.

Holden wrote: 'A committee, composed of Sir David L. Salomons, Bart,

Above left *In 1904 the Association of
Licensed Motor Manufacturers, who were
attempting to obtain a monopoly over the
American motor industry using the
'master patent' of G.B. Selden, who
claimed to have invented the motor car in
1877, brought a suit against Henry Ford.
In defence (the hearing dragged on until
January 1911), Ford had this little car
built, powered by a replica of Lenoir's
engine of 1863, to prove 'prior invention'.*

Right *The retrospective exhibition at the
1907 Paris Salon, with (1) an 1886 De
Dion Bouton steam carriage, (2) an 1885
De Dion tricycle, (3) an 1898 Jeantaud
electric, (4) an 1898 Darracq-Bollée and
(5) a general view of the exhibition.*

(Vice Chairman), Lord Montagu, Professor Healey Shaw, FRS, Mr W. Worby Beaumont, MICE, Mr Mervyn O'Gorman, MIEE and Mr James Swinburn, FRS, has been formed for the purpose of making this collection. I have undertaken the chairmanship of this committee, and Mr Claude Johnson, who was the first secretary of the Automobile Club of Great Britain and Ireland (now the Royal Automobile Club), has undertaken to act as honorary secretary.

'In the whole history of engineering nothing has been so striking as the rapidity with which the design of automobiles has advanced, and it is desired, in the historical collection above referred to, to have the earliest forms of motor vehicles and subsequent forms made prior to the 1904 which will illustrate the development of the motor car.'

The historic cars were housed in a large court to the left of the Court of Honour, close by the main entrance to the exhibition. The oldest vehicle on display was Colonel R.E.B. Crompton's steam carriage, *Blue Belle*, on which he had begun work at the age of 16. He subsequently took *Blue Belle* to India, where he pioneered the use of steam traction in military service. It was claimed that *Blue Belle* was the first road vehicle to incorporate differential gearing in its transmission. Only the chassis of *Blue Belle* was displayed at Shepherds Bush, and it was noted that it had 'a water tube boiler with vertical water tubes, almost identical with many forms of boilers now in use, the boiler being supported on a rocking shaft. The two-cylinder horizontal engine looks today as though it had left the workshops but a few minutes ago. This carriage was built in 1861, and was, we believe, running as late as 1875'.

Then there was the early steam tricycle built by Arthur Bateman of Greenwich in 1881, and shown that year at the Stanley Cycle Show in the Holborn Town Hall. A visitor to Shepherds Bush noted: 'This machine is interesting from the fact that the action taken by the authorities in connection with it proved the bar to the advancement of road locomotion for many years. It was declared to be a steam carriage as prohibited by the Highways Act, and therefore could not be driven unless the wheels were four inches wide, unless it had three men in attendance, one of whom must carry a red flag, and the pace was confined to a maximum of 4 mph. Mr Bateman was fined one shilling for breaking the law, and on appealing to a higher court the conviction was affirmed. By this chuckle-headed decision, therefore, our friends across the Channel were given the huge start in the motor industry which we can hardly yet be said to have overtaken. The little two-cylinder horizontal engine was set above the water tube boiler, and drove the nearside rubber-tyred wheel of the tricycle by means of bevelled gearing'.

Next to the Bateman was J.H. Knight's 1895 car, powered by a modified forward gas engine. Originally built as a three-wheeler, the Knight car was subsequently rebuilt with four wheels in the interests of stability. There was a 6 hp Belsize car, said to have been built in 1898, by Marshall & Company of Clayton, Manchester, forerunners of Belsize Motors. The Marshall car, a copy of the French Hurtu car, was itself a close copy of the Benz. The original Lanchester car, built in 1896, was shown, though its original tiller steering had been replaced by a wheel. The second Lanchester, dating from 1897, still retained the side tiller. Also there was an early James & Browne 6 hp twin-cylinder prototype of 1899, which had been driven from London to Solihull shortly after it was built, which had a curious chain transmission with two forward speeds and separate friction clutches.

Wolseley had lent two of its earliest cars, an 1898 three-wheeler and the first four-wheeled car, completed in 1899, both cars being designed by Herbert Austin. The four-wheeler ran in the 1900 Thousand Miles Trial, and in 1970 the 84-year-old St John Nixon used this car for his own personal commemoration of the 70th Anniversary of the Trial, in which he retraced the route round England, ignoring a celebratory rally by the Veteran Car Club. Mr Nixon died shortly after he had triumphantly completed the trip.

Two other Shepherds Bush exhibits with connections with the Thousand Miles Trial were an Ariel Quad, a spindly machine with a fair amount of motorcycle in its make-up, and a 3½ hp New Orleans car (a British built copy of the Belgian Vivinus car, and virtually indistinguishable from the French Piéper). A 6 hp Daimler twin-cylinder of 1900 was described as accentuating the enormous advance made in motor car design in so short a time. 'Short wheelbase, high, clumsy looking, inartistic in every way, these machines when first put upon the road were the marvel and admiration of the pioneer motorists of the day'.

French manufacturers had sent some historic vehicles: De Dion Bouton had provided not only an 1885 steam tricycle, but also their first four-wheeled steam carriage, completed in their factory in a house in the Rue Pergolese, Paris, later the same year. Serpollet had sent the very first Serpollet vehicle, a three-wheeler built in 1887. Hippolyte Panhard had lent an 1891 2½ hp twin-cylinder Panhard while the 'Auto-Palace' Garage had lent a mid-engined 1892 Panhard whose twin-cylinder vertical engine drove a transverse gearbox.

Two rare early French petrol cars were the 1897 Berliet and a cabriolet built by Landry et Beyroux, also known as MLB. A De Dion motorcycle of 1895 and an 1897 single-cylinder Bollée voiturette with wicker forecarriage, said to be the vehicle on which famous racing drivers Charles Jarrott and S.F. Edge had made many of their first motor journeys, were included in the French exhibits, as were an 1897 twin horsepower Panhard, an 1899 6 hp single-cylinder Darracq-Bollée with a two seated body and an underfloor single-cylinder engine with the 'breech of the cylinder approaching the front axle'. There was one of the early 1¾ hp single-cylinder Renaults, with handle-bar steering, the curious racing Vallée, *La Pantoufle*, with a wedge-shaped body, built for Dr Lehwess (who in 1902 made an ill-fated attempt to drive round the world in a huge Panhard motor caravan, *Le Passe-partout*). Of more modern appearance were the rear-engined 1901 4½ hp single-cylinder De Dion, and the twin-cylinder 7-10 hp Panhard of the same year.

The only German cars on display included an 1894 twin-cylinder Daimler, the 1889 Steel-wheeler from the same company and an 1895 Lutzmann (possibly the car entered in veteran car events today by Bernard Garrett of Limpsfield, Surrey). Benz had provided two of their early cars and the Belgian firm of Germain showed a 6 hp twin-cylinder car built under Daimler-Levassor patents which was identical to the German Phönix Daimler. When the collection was dispersed at the end of the exhibition, the motoring press called for the establishment of a permanent exhibition of historic motor cars.

The first proposal for a motor museum came from Edmund Dangerfield, proprietor of *The Motor* in England. In 1909, contrary to his previously held view that faith in the future implied discarding the past, Dangerfield demanded that historic old cars should be preserved and that a permanent museum should be set up to preserve the earliest motor vehicles. His staff were set the task of discovering as many historic early cars as possible in order that a museum should be set up, and the establishment of The Motor Museum was announced in the magazine on January 23 1912. At first, the Motor Museum took over the premises of Waring & Gillow in Oxford Street, London, as temporary head-quarters. Under the patronage of HRH The Duke of Teck, the museum was opened by Sir David Salomons, one of the first British motorists, at the end of May 1912. It remained open for six months, during which time the general public were admitted at a cost of a shilling, though members of the RAC and AA were given free admission.

At the end of the six months the exhibits were transferred to what was planned to be their permanent home in the Crystal Palace, and the museum was again opened by the Duke of Teck in February 1913. However, when war began on August 4 1914, the Crystal Palace was taken over by the Admiralty and the historical cars were either returned to their donors or taken to store in West London. Some were abandoned on a disused lot near Charing Cross Station and eventually vanished. Fortunately some of the exhibits survive today though they are widely dispersed around Britain. The earliest car in the Motor Museum was Crompton's *Blue Belle*.

The oldest petrol car in the display was the 1891 Panhard-Levassor, one of the first cars with a forward engine produced by this company, owned by Abbé Gavois, who had bought it when Curé of the village of Bellay-Saint-Léonard, in 1895. He had bought it from the Mayor of Troyes for 1,800 francs, and by the time it went on exhibition in London it had been in daily service for over 20 years. In 1911 it had won the Gold Medal at 'the competition of primitive motor cars'. It was an exceedingly primitive vehicle having iron shod tyres, hot tube ignition and a curious 'brush clutch' consisting of a brush with metal bristles geared to a plate rigidly attached to the motor shaft; a second plate on the trans-mission shaft had shallow teeth cut in its face, and, to quote the museum catalogue: 'By moving this plate until it comes in contact with the bristles, an efficient drive is obtained'. In 1928 the Abbé was reported to be planning to sell his car to raise the money to build a chapel devoted to St Christopher, patron saint of travellers. There were two other Panhards in the exhibition, one of 1892, loaned by Hippolyte Panhard, the other an 1897 model which had been modified to incorporate wheel steering instead of the standard tiller.

What was claimed to be Britain's oldest four-wheeled petrol car was another significant exhibit; completed in 1894 by a Walthamstow engineer named Fred Bremer, this tiny 3 hp car was inspired by the Benz and still survives, in the Walthamstow Museum, to which Bremer left it in the 1920s. It was restored to running order by a Veteran Car Club member named John Trott and success-fully completed the London to Brighton Run in the mid 1960s.

Other early vehicles on show included John Henry Knight's 1 hp car, an 1894/5 Cannstatt Daimler Victoria, an 1898 Darracq Bollée, with belt drive and centre pivot steering, an 1898 Coventry Motette (an Anglicised version of the Léon Bollée tri-car), and a French-built genuine Bollée, fitted with a wicker-work fore-carriage. The three earliest Wolseleys (still in existence) were on loan from the manufacturers: another vehicle which still survives was an 1897 Bersey electric motor cab, today displayed at Beaulieu. It was said to have been the first motor cab in London, and to have been ridden in by the then Prince of Wales (later Edward VII) from Marlborough House to Buckingham Palace and back in November 1897.

There was a clutch of vehicles based on the Benz—a 1900 Marshall dogcart,

An 'Historical Exhibit' of early cars was part of the 1930 Olympia Motor Show. Remarked The Autocar: *'Very odd the old cars look, cars which, in their day were every bit as much the most wonderful examples of the latest designs for speedy travel as the strangely contrasting 1931 chassis'. This is a 1903 Swift, with a 1904 Sunbeam 12 hp behind.*

an 1898 Star dogcart and an 1897 Arnold Benz, probably the sole surviving example of this make which is today preserved by its original manufacturers, Arnold's of East Peckham, Kent. A genuine Benz was exhibited, too, dating from 1899 and having been rescued from a copse in Berkshire by an 'inspector'. The car, which had been extensively modified, had been reunited with its power unit, which at some stage had been removed to provide the power for an electric lighting installation in Hampshire. The curious four-seater side-entrance body is almost certainly later than 1899, and was in a somewhat decrepit state; this was hardly surprising as at the time of the car's discovery, 'it was forming an apparently comfortable residence for a healthy community of poultry'.

The Scottish motor industry was represented by the first Argyll car, powered by an MMC engine and dating from 1899, while Albion had donated one of their curious varnished wood dogcarts. There was also a primitive cyclecar, said to have been built in 1900 by Henry Sturmey, founding editor of *The Autocar*, and powered by a $2\frac{3}{4}$ hp aircooled motorcycle engine and three-speed epicyclic gearing. Other vehicles on display included a 1901 12/14 hp belt-driven Delahaye presented by Sir J.H.A. MacDonald, a 1901 Gardner Serpollet and a 1901 6 hp White steam car, a 1900 Cleveland electric, an 1895 Peugeot, the first and second Lanchester cars, an 1898 6 hp Coventry Daimler, a curious 1897 Clément, and, apparently, an early Clément-Panhard.

Early steam and petrol motorcycles were also displayed; bridging the gap between cars and motorcycles was the fearsome Pennington 'Torpedo Autocar', a three-wheeled monstrosity then preserved by C.A. 'Bath Road' Smith, the former racing cyclist who kept the White Lion on the Portsmouth Road at Cobham, Surrey, an inn much frequented by pioneer motorists, and featured in the novel *The Lightning Conductor*.

A remarkable French museum

For the connoisseur of the eccentric, a visit to the National French Museum at Compiègne is indispensable. Housed in a former Napoleonic château, the

Despite its archaic appearance the 1878 Bollée La Mancelle, *preserved at Compiègne, is amazingly modern in concept, with an engine at the front driving the rear wheels and independent front suspension by transverse leaf springs.*

transport museum at Compiègne covers road and rail vehicles of all kinds, from primitive horse-drawn sleds to motor cars. It is typically French in that the majority of the exhibits are unrestored, having been donated to the collection many years ago. Many of the larger exhibits are kept in a roofed-over courtyard, just by the museum entrance; it is here that some of the rarer vehicles are on display.

There is full evidence of the remarkable genius of the Bollée family in the shape of *La Mancelle*, which Bollée *père* designed in 1878, and which was intended for limited series production. Had Bollée been as astute a salesman as he was capable as an engineer, the subsequent history of motoring could well have been different. For *La Mancelle*, 20 years ahead of its time, had its engine mounted at the front under a bonnet, driving the rear wheels through a propellor shaft and side chains. Even more remarkable, it was fitted with a very sophisticated form of front suspension by parallel transverse springs. It was still considered *avant garde* when a similar system was adopted by the Sizaire brothers in the 1920s. Add to this wheel steering—most of the early petrol cars still used the obsolete and unsatisfactory tiller—and stylish, if massive, lines and you have perhaps the most significant vehicle of the age of steam.

Next to *La Mancelle* is a steam carriage created in 1883 by Bollée's son, also named Amédée, to the order of the Marquis de Broc. Though it was built some six years later than *La Mancelle*, the vehicle has a far more antiquated appearance. Amédée *fils* was certainly capable of advanced design—he built a neat and attractive light steam-powered two-seater for his own use which would not have looked out of place 15 years after its construction, but one suspects that with the carriage for the Marquis he was working under orders, and executed the commission very much with his tongue in his cheek. Certainly for sheer massiveness and incongruity of appearance the de Broc carriage has few peers in the history of motoring. It stands perhaps 14 feet high, has a seat on the roof, complete with hood and windscreen in the manner of a diligence type of stagecoach, and creates an overwhelmingly ponderous impression. It seems to

This 1896 Bollée at Compiègne was one of the first shaft-driven cars, with a transmission system of fiendish ingenuity. Note, too, the channel iron chassis frame, at a time when most manufacturers were using wood or cycle tubing for their chassis.

combine all the worst design features of railway and horse-drawn road carriages, yet the overall image is irresistably appealing.

Elsewhere at Compiègne, other significant motor vehicles are preserved. In what appears to have been the kitchen of the old château is a group of historic vehicles possibly without equal in the world. Some of them, certainly, have a slightly woebegone look, for they are just as they were brought into the museum when their useful lives were over. That should not disguise the fact that in the one room are: the world's first internal combustion saloon car; the first practical shaft drive petrol car; the first vehicle to exceed 60 mph (100 km/h) and a number of other unique machines including an extremely early Gobron-Brillié (with its opposed-piston engine that could run on 'whisky, brandy or any other good quality spirit'), Panhard and De Dion Bouton vehicles. One of the Compiègne's De Dions is a steam tricycle built in De Dion's original factory.

The first saloon car, a little single-cylinder Renault, has lost its tyres over the years, and sustained some mechanical modifications; nevertheless, no one had built such a small car with enclosed accommodation for the driver before. It is possible that the Renault may have been ante-dated by an Audibert et Lavirotte, from Lyon, but it is certainly the earliest saloon car to survive.

Shaft drive to the rear axle, as opposed to chains or belts, was first successfully used by Amédée Bollée *fils* in 1896, but on a system vastly different from that used by just about every other car maker since; Bollée's shafts ran outside the vehicle, driving the hub of each rear wheel through a worm gearing. The system is so complex that one wonders how Bollée ever managed to devise it. Nevertheless, shortly after that Bollée built a series of remarkable streamlined racing cars known as *Torpilleurs*, which not only had the first monobloc four-cylinder engines with twin carburettors, but also made use of underslung rear suspension, aluminium coachwork and a rear mounted engine. Their low build was their undoing; the carburettors sucked in dust from the road which choked the engines.

And the first car to exceed 100 km/h, the electrically driven *La Jamais*

Contente, was designed by the Belgian racing driver, Camille Jenatzy, in 1899, with the aid of the Fulmen battery company. For its day, *La Jamais Contente* is amazingly advanced in concept, for its bodyshell is pointed like a bullet, and it rides on very small wheels to keep the centre of gravity as low as possible. Unfortunately much of the effect of the streamlining must have been nullified by the fact that the driver sat on top of the body with only his legs inside. On May 1 1899 Jenatzy took the car to a straight stretch of road which cut across the Achères sewage farm, to the west of Paris, and, 'with a subdued sound, like the rustling of wings', he travelled faster than any motorist had ever travelled up to that date, convincingly shattering the previous world speed record, established by the Comte de Chasseloup-Laubat, driving a Jeantaud electric, who had taken 39 seconds to cover the kilometre. Jenatzy took 34 seconds at a speed of 105 km/h. Both Jenatzy and Jeantaud were to have unhappy ends; Jenatzy, imitating a wild boar as a practical joke on a hunting party, was shot by one of his guests, while Jeantaud committed suicide when the demand for electric vehicles ceased in 1907.

More museums

Really early road vehicles are rare; there is a long gap from the Cugnot preserved in Paris to the next oldest road carriage, the remains of a Goldsworthy Gurney steam drag preserved in the Glasgow museum of transport. This particular vehicle was brought to Scotland in March 1831 in order to try out an Edinburgh-Glasgow service which had been proposed by a Mr Ward, using six such drags. Goldsworthy Gurney, who was subsequently knighted for his work in installing central heating in the Houses of Parliament, had built an elaborate steamer with which he drove from London to Bath in 1828, accompanied by many breakdowns. Deciding that the future lay with a lighter, simpler machine, he developed a steam drag, the forerunner of the private car, a light carriage which could be used to haul a horse carriage if desired. The 1831 version differed only from the prototype in having spring suspension and a modified boiler.

It seems that the drag sent to Scotland made only one successful run, from Glasgow to Paisley and Renfrew and back. A later trip from Edinburgh to Glasgow lasted three days. Finally, early in June 1831, the boiler exploded on the outskirts of Glasgow. The Glasgow museum preserves the wheel-less chassis, no parts of the boiler or superstructure having survived. The Glasgow museum also preserves examples of Scotland's contribution to the motor car industry, including vehicles by Argyll, Albion, Arrol-Johnson, Galloway and Beardmore.

But the greatest surviving testimonial to the age of the steam carriage is preserved in Turin's Museo dell'Automobile Carlo Biscaretti di Ruffia. This is the 1854 Bordino, built by Virginio Bordino, an officer in the engineers from Piedmont, who during a period of study in England had built in 1836 a steam carriage closely modelled on that of Macerone and subsequently, in 1852, had built a three-wheeled calèche, possibly using parts of the first machine. But in 1854, in the military arsenal of Turin, he built his third and most magnificent steam carriage, which is the one which survives today in perfect order. In concept, the Bordino is of the 1830s rather than the 1850s, being a huge landau with a rear mounted coke fired boiler and an underfloor, twin-cylinder, horizontal steam engine acting directly on the rear crank axle. In service, the

The Compiègne museum houses both the first car to exceed 100 km/h, the torpedo-shaped La Jamais Contente *and the first saloon car, the 1900 Renault coupé.*

Bordino was found to consume 30 kilogrammes of coke an hour and to achieve a speed of 8 km/h on the level.

The Turin museum's origins date back to 1932, when Cesare Coria Gatti, Roberto Biscaretti di Ruffia, Giuseppe Acuitis, Giuseppe di Miceli and especially Carlo Biscaretti di Ruffia, a founder of Fiat, proposed forming a motor car museum in Turin. Count Carlo Biscaretti had devoted his lifetime to the history of the motor vehicle, and was an accomplished artist whose work was used to advertise products such as Michelin tyres and Itala cars. He assembled a collection of technically and historically significant vehicles which were temporarily put on display at Turin's municipal stadium.

In 1956, the Italian motor industry and the Agnelli family, which controls Fiat, became convinced that this steadily growing collection of vehicles was worthy of support and needed a permanent—and appropriate—home. They underwrote the construction of a large, modern museum building on a plot of land donated by the city of Turin. The construction of the new permanent motor car museum began in 1957, and Count Biscaretti was named the first president of the museum. However, he died in 1959 before the building was complete.

The museum was opened to the public on November 3 1960, and named Museo del Automobile Carlo Biscaretti di Ruffia in honour of the man who had been its greatest driving force. The ultra-modern museum building, which contains over 300 major items, was designed by the architect, Amedeo Albertini. Apart from the Bordino, perhaps the Turin museum's greatest treasure is the 1907 35/45 hp Itala which, driven by Prince Scipione Borghese, won the 16,000 kilometre Peking to Paris race in 44 days' running time.

At Dearborn, Michigan, the Henry Ford Museum exhibits a comprehensive collection of vehicles in an eight-acre building with the world's largest parquet floor. Historical highlights of the collection include an 1865 Roper steam carriage, one of the oldest existing fully operative cars in the United States. America's first automobile offered for public sale, an 1896 Duryea motor wagon (the only survivor of 13 sold that year) and Henry Ford's first vehicle, the 1896 Quadricycle, are collection highlights. Other early vehicles on show are the 1903 Model A, Ford's first mass-produced car: the Selden Auto Buggy, built in 1905 as a court test of Selden's 1877 patent with which he attempted to monopolise the US car industry, and a 1903 Cadillac, built in the first full year of that company.

The variations in design and advances in development are apparent throughout the collection, as evidenced by such cars as a 1904 Model L Packard (the museum exhibits the only surviving model of the 198 originally produced), 1931 Bugatti Royale (one of eight of these models designed to be the largest and most luxurious cars ever built), 1931 Duesenberg cabriolet (America's premier classic), the innovative 1948 Tucker and a sporty 1956 Ford Thunderbird.

Many vehicles in the museum's collection have strong connections with history and famous individuals. President Taft's Baker Electric is in the collection, as well as Franklin Delano Roosevelt's 1939 'Sunshine Special' Lincoln and the Presidential Lincoln used by Presidents Truman and Eisenhower. The transportation collection also features personal cars of J.P. Morgan, Walter P. Chrysler, Charles A. Lindbergh, Thomas A. Edison and exhibits the 1940 Chrysler Crown Imperial which served as New York City's parade car for many years.

Racing cars are represented by such models as the 1902 Ford '999', driven by Barney Oldfield, and a sleek 1955 Mercedes-Benz 300 SLR, which was driven to a sports car world championship by Stirling Moss, the only one of its type on exhibit outside the Mercedes-Benz museum in Germany.

Commercial vehicles also feature: an 1898 Riker electric truck and a 1906

Below *Henry Ford's office in Detroit, photographed around 1914. The office itself has been preserved in the Henry Ford Museum.*
Above right *Recreating early car manufacturing methods—a team of old-car experts reassembles a 1903 Ford Model A in a replica of the original Ford factory on Mack Avenue, Detroit, part of the Greenfield Village museum at Dearborn. This was part of the worldwide celebrations of the 75th Anniversary of the Ford Motor Company in 1978.*
Right *These elegant buildings, inspired by Independence Hall in Philadelphia, form the frontage of the Ford Museum in Dearborn, officially known as the Edison Institute.*
Below right *An early photograph of the Henry Ford Museum at Dearborn, with Benz cars in the foreground, plus part of the world's biggest parquet floor—eight acres of it! The museum entered the 1980s with the road transport section redesigned into 'themes', and some of the cars being sold off as being 'of little historic interest' (including Henry Ford's 1913 Minerva tourer and a 1909 Renault Town Car).*

This is one of the first 800 Model T Fords built, at the end of 1908; only these cars had a second lever to obtain reverse. The subsequent 16 million-odd Model Ts all had a pedal-operated reverse and, indeed, a conversion kit was offered to 'update' the earliest cars to this specification (Henry Ford Museum, Dearborn).

Rapid bus are two of the many earlier vehicles on exhibit. The Henry Ford Museum Transportation Collection also includes exhibits of automotive parts and accessories. These include the world's first three-colour, four-direction traffic light, designed by Superintendent W.L. Potts of the Detroit Police Department and installed at the intersection of Woodward Avenue and Fort Street, Detroit, Michgan, in October 1920. An impressive collection of automotive brass, Lalique crystal radiator ornaments and other transportation-related items, including the first visible-display gasoline dispensing station, complete the museum's world famous collection.

Car factories

As you drive from Glasgow to Loch Lomond, you pass through the town of Alexandria. One of the dominant features of the town is a huge terracotta building, which was standing empty at the beginning of 1980, yet represented one of the most ambitious chapters in the early days of the British or, rather, Scottish motor industry. Argyll Motors Limited, who started production at the turn of the century in Bridgeton, Glasgow, under the direction of Alec Govan, building close copies of the contemporary Renault voiturette, began work in 1905 on a 'motor factory which for completeness and magnitude should stand alone'.

The Autocar waxed eloquent about the project: 'As a building it is a beautiful building, and as a factory it is everything which foresight and experience could make it. Nothing has been omitted which can tend to add to the comfort of the work people. The sanitary arrangements are above criticism, and the space devoted to lavatory and cloakroom accommodation for the work people occupies as much ground and must have cost as much money as many a factory complete'.

In fact, every workman had his own numbered wash basin, and the use of

Preserved by the Henry Ford Museum, this 1929 Ford Model A coupé was Henry Ford's personal car. Painted in black (what else?), the car has a special storage socket in the rear window shelf to carry a bottle of Vichy water, which Henry favoured for his health at that time (Henry Ford Museum, Dearborn).

marble surfaces was a luxury which few motor factories before or since have managed to equal. No wonder that *The Autocar* commented, 'As its fame spreads among the mechanics in the motor engineering world, we have no doubt that it will be regarded as a privilege to work in such a perfectly laid out manufactory'.

Architecturally, the outstanding feature of the Alexandria Works was—and is—the terracotta administration building facing the main road. When it was opened, on June 26 1906, its three gilt domes glinting in the sunlight, the building seemed more than a little grandiose compared with the size of the contemporary car market. Govan countered such criticism with the statement that: 'Perhaps our front is a little in advance of our requirements, but it is intentionally so, as the plan is that it shall still be adequate for administration purposes when the factory behind it has grown to twice or even three times its present size. We are looking ahead a little and I think our profit on the land warrants our so doing. Already the land on which the works stand has been paid for, and a profit of £40,000 made on the surplus ground'. Certainly the construction of Alexandria was an impressive feat of civil engineering. The building had swallowed up 85,000 tons of materials, and had been built inside 14 months from the breaking of the first ground. It had beaten the contemporary bricklaying record, the stonework record and the record for the installation of machine tools.

The 300 guests who were present at the formal opening ceremony of Alexandria, when Lord Montagu of Beaulieu opened the door of the works were, in the words of a contemporary account, 'astounded'. It must have been an impressive occasion. 'A pleasing feature of this function was the interest of the work people who evidently appreciated the privilege of working in a factory in which everything that modern science and mechanics and hygiene could do had been done for their benefit and comfort. A few minutes before the opening ceremony, they had been released for their midday meal, and every man and boy had hastened from his shop to the front of the works so that he might be present'. Few of the guests, as they sat down to lunch in the great entertainment hall at the south end of the building, can have foreseen the rapid decline of Argyll. The company had proved too optimistic about the future and were a spent force by the outbreak of the Great War. Though they survived through the 1920s, Argyll were but a shadow of their former selves and never regained the pre-eminence they had had before the opening of Alexandria.

Incidentally, to mark the opening of the building, Alexander Govan was presented with a rose bowl in chased silver with a picture of the works 'beautifully engraved' upon it, as well as a clock and a pair of vases; it would be interesting to know whether any of these items survive today. If the Argyll factory had been to grandiose for its own good, a couple of years earlier a more modest plant had been opened in London which was to produce some of Britain's finest cars during the next three decades. This was the Talbot Motor works in Barlby Road, Ladbroke Grove, nowadays owned by the car dealers Warwick Wright (founded, incidentally, by a famous racing driver of pre-First World War).

It was in 1903 that a syndicate was set up to import the French Clement cars into Britain, headed by the Earl of Shrewsbury and Talbot. The establishment of the Clement-Talbot company, backed by both English and French capital 'expended under expert English and French advice', was announced at the annual dinner of the British Automobile Syndicate held in November 1903 at London's Hotel Cecil. Shortly afterwards work began on a 5¼-acre site in Ladbroke Grove, Notting Hill, an extensive, soundly constructed, and thoroughly well-equipped automobile works. The work was carried out under the supervision of Charles Garrard, who had worked for many years in France with Adolphe Clement and who had built his first horseless carriage—propelled by electricity—as early as 1893, in Birmingham. Garrard had, in fact, joined Clement in 1888, when Clement was making his first inroads into the cycle industry.

Below left *With the revival of the Talbot marque in 1978, the wheel has gone full circle for the Clement-Talbot works in London's Ladbroke Grove, for it is now occupied by Warwick Wright, the London Talbot agents. Opened in 1903 to build Talbot cars, the factory was to undergo extensive restoration to its original state in the early 1980s.*

Right *This huge plaque on the wall of the old Talbot works would originally have read 'Clement-Talbot Automobile Works', but when Talbot became part of the Sunbeam-Talbot-Darracq combine after the Great War, the inscription was changed. Fortunately, 'Sunbeam' had the same number of letters as 'Clement'. . ...*

The frontage of the Clement-Talbot works, a red sandstone building, was imposing and was entered through a porte-cochère which had a carriage sweep running off what was then Edinburgh Road (now Barlby Road), a specially made highway leading in front of the building. The entrance hall—also known as the Grand Hall—had a mosaic pavement and 'rich and tasteful marble decorations'. It doubled as a showroom, where visitors could see finished cars, chassis, sectioned working models, 'interesting relics' and accessories. The hall was intended as a past and present museum.

To the right of the hall was the administration wing which included the drawing offices, which *The Autocar* coyly referred to as the 'germ-hive of the whole works and their output'. To the left of the hall, a pair of plate glass swing doors gave on to a balcony in the power house, which contained four engines, three 200 hp units and a 14 hp auxiliary engine. The 14 hp engine not only started the main engines, but also ran the pilot lighting in the evening and also provided light for the furnace men on night shift in the metallurgical, toughening and annealing departments, as well as running a number of 'self-caring for' automatic machines. At the far end of this wing was the stock room while below it was a workshop and the mill-wrights store. A separate building housed the actual production facilities, where the chassis were erected.

The plant, which even in its first form had provision for an extension of a third as much factory space again, was circled by a test track on which chassis could be tried out before being fitted with bodies from the firm's own coach-building operation which was housed in a series of small buildings down one side of the entire site. At the back of the site were the case hardening and smiths shops and the testing house, positioned as far away from the main plant as possible to preserve the main building as much as possible from the noise and inconvenience of the processes carried out in these shops. In the testing shop motors were tested on water turbines. The engines had been specially built for the Clement-Talbot firm by 'those eminent motor builders Messrs Willans &

Robinson of Rugby and will each be three-cylinders inverted vertical gas engines coupled direct to continuous current dynamos'.

Ingenuity was evident in the method used to heat the factory. The water from the cylinder jackets passed into jackets round the exhaust pipes and then to a superheater, which could be boosted by gas burners if required. The hot water was circulated through pipes to the radiators in the rooms of the administration building, while a primitive form of air conditioning was provided by enforced draught fans which fed filtered air through galvanised conduits beneath the radiators 'in such volume that the air in each apartment is completely changed every twenty minutes. The temperature in each room can be varied at will by the manipulation of the radiators. Thus all the waste heat from the engines is most economically utilised'. The gas plant which produced the gas on which the engines ran provided the heat for the works; a bank of pipes was in contact with the flames from the producer gas furnace and air was forced through these by a fan to warm the factory.

Work on the factory proceeded steadily and by mid-September 1904 it was practically complete. The ebullient works manager, Danny Weigel (later builder of cars under his own name, including the first, if unsuccessful, straight-eight Grand Prix car), took *The Autocar*'s representative on a tour of the factory; having noticed that a large number of the very latest English and American machine tools and the first of the huge three-cylinder gas engines were already in position, the journalist waxed lyrical. 'The care and forethought given in the design by the architect to the comfort and health of the work people are beyond all praise, and from our considerable acquaintance with metal works of various designs, we do not hesitate to say that few, if any, engineering works in the United Kingdom can vie with the Talbot works in these respects. The building, which comprises the entrance hall, showroom and offices, is admirable to a degree both inside and out, the entrance hall being so tasteful and artistic in design and lavish in material that it might be the vestibule to an art gallery storing the art treasures of a world.'

It is remarkable indeed that the Talbot works has survived. It was here that the first motor car ever to cover 100 miles in an hour was built; it was here that the great Swiss engineer, Georges Roesch, designed highly efficient sports cars in the late 1920s and early 1930s which had few rivals for speed and stamina. But when the collapse of the Sunbeam-Talbot-Darracq combine dragged this admirable company down in the mid-1930s, it was acquired by the Rootes Group, who were hungry to build a motor industry empire and already had taken over Humber, Hillman and Singer. The once proud name of Talbot was applied to some inferior motor cars, like the Talbot Ten which was no more than a worked-over Hillman Minx concealed beneath a Thrupp & Maberley coachbuilt body and powered by a humdrum sidevalve engine instead of Roesch's lively overhead valve unit with the rockers, actuated by knitting needle-like push rods, pivoting delicately on knife edges. So highly regarded had the name Talbot been on both sides of the Channel that, when in 1979 the French Peugeot group acquired the failing Chrysler-Europe operation that had absorbed the dying Rootes company as well as Simca of Paris, it decided to rename its product Talbot.

London has other notable former car plants: the former Bentley factory in Oxgate Lane, Cricklewood, is now occupied by the accessory firm, Smiths Industries, while the Kingsbury factory, originally the home of the Kingsbury

Junior light car, was taken over in 1925 by Vanden Plas. They not only built many bodies for Bentley, but also leased part of their factory for Bentley's service department. This London branch company outlived its Belgian parent, but at the end of 1979, BL, the owners of Vanden Plas, announced that the Kingsbury works were to be shut down and their operations transferred to the Jaguar factory in Coventry.

In Tinsley, Sheffield, the former Sheffield-Simplex factory still exists, occupied today by the Ever-Ready electric company. Built in 1906 at a cost of £10,990, the Sheffield-Simplex works were backed by Earl Fitzwilliam, a peer whose stately home at Wentworth Woodhouse was said to be Britain's biggest private dwelling. It was at Tinsley that the famous 'gearbox-less' 45 hp six-cylinder Sheffield-Simplex was built. A 45 hp car ran from Land's End to John O'Groats without stopping its engine all the way on its 3:1 direct drive (except for quick recourse to its 'emergency low' when baulked by a slow vehicle). One of these splendid cars was recently discovered in Australia, and is now being restored in England.

It is possible to find historic motor car factories still, though in Coventry, where so many factories were once situated, wartime bombing destroyed many of them. One of the casualties of the war was the birthplace of the British motor industry, the famous Coventry Motor Mills, a disused cotton mill taken over by the egregious Harry J. Lawson to house his grandiose scheme to monopolise the British motor industry. The main part of the Motor Mills was occupied from early 1896 by the Motor Manufacturing Company, with the Daimler Motor Company in a lesser building round the back. A former employee of the Motor Mills, whom I interviewed in the 1960s, told me that there was little difference between the products of these two main components of Lawson's empire, apart from the manufacturer's plate fitted to each vehicle. The Motor Manufacturing Company concentrated on body building, while the Daimler Company was concerned with the mechanical components of the vehicles.

The upper storeys of the Motor Mills were occupied by other satellites of Lawson, such as the American 'motor charlatan' Edward Joel Pennington, who, in exchange for a vast payment for patent rights, produced a handful of mechanically unsound designs ranging from a crude motorcycle to the abortive Raft Victoria, a front-wheel-drive, rear-wheel-steer monstrosity with final drive by rope, which amazingly attracted many orders when it was publically exhibited in 1897. An early example was driven by Hubert W. Egerton in a proposed run from Coventry to London; having used 72 spark plugs to get from Coventry to Nuneaton, Egerton abandoned the unequal struggle.

Some of the older buildings in Coventry survive; a few years ago part of the old Lea Francis works in Much Park Street were still standing; as these were half timbered mediaeval buildings which had been adapted to the motor age, they must have been the oldest premises ever used to build motor cars (though one ephemeral Canadian manufacturer built his cars in a converted church). The Lea Francis building was all that remains of a much larger factory gutted by fire in 1966 and demolished.

In nearby Wolverhampton, the Clyno works were certainly still in evidence in 1967, when I took my 1927 Clyno to meet some of the men who had helped to build it. The Clyno factory in Pelham Street seemed amazingly small to have built over 300 cars a week at the peak of Clyno's success in 1926-7, before an ill-considered move to brand new premises at Bushbury (later taken over by the

Left *One of the great monuments to the Edwardian age of motoring is the Royal Automobile Club in London's Pall Mall. Designed by Mewes and Davis and E. Keynes Purchase, it was built on the site of the old War Office between 1908-11 by the Building Construction Company at a cost of over £100,000. On the pediment is depicted a Cupid in a car.*

Below right *The Benz factory in Waldhoff-strasse, Mannheim, where Benz cars and engines were built between 1886-1908.*

machine tool firm, Alfred Herbert) caused their downfall. At that time, the Clyno factory which had started life as a nut and bolt works owned by the Stevens family of AJS fame, was owned by the Midlands Metal Spinning Company, turning out saucepans and kitchen utensils.

When William Morris went into production with Morris cars, he took over the old priory at Cowley, Oxford. Morris's office in the building was preserved as a relic of the past. In 1904, the Horley Motor & Engineering Company, of Balcombe Road, Horley, Surrey, marketed their first car, an 8 hp single-cylinder which, by 1905, was selling at the remarkably low price of 100 guineas. In the 1960s the engineering company which took over the former premises, in which the Horley car was built, discovered, when they were installing new machinery, a nameplate from a Horley car buried in the earth floor of the works.

Grandiose plants like those of Argyll and Talbot were well enough in their way, but the man who created the first truly modern automobile factory was Albert Kahn, who in some 40 years of activity for all America's major motor manufacturers produced some two billion dollars' worth of factories at 1940's values. Kahn was the son of a Jewish rabbi who had emigrated to America from Germany via Luxemburg in 1880. Albert, aged 12, worked as a waiter at night and as an office boy for a firm of architects in the day, and decided to become an architect. His first boss fired him because he had no apparent aptitude for drawing and also because he smelt of horses, from working in his father's stable every morning before work. He was befriended by an elderly German sculptor and art teacher, Julius Melchers, who not only taught him in his drawing school but found a job for him in an architectural office. At the age of 21 he won a $500 travelling scholarship offered by the magazine *The American Architect* and travelled in Europe. In America he began designing houses, but was laid off in 1895 when a depression curtailed house building in Detroit. He went into partnership with two colleagues, but one left to head the architectural school at Cornell University and the other died, so Albert filled their places with his five younger brothers as they graduated from school.

Initially, Kahn earned his living designing small houses and remodelling old houses, but in 1903 he obtained two significant commissions. One was as architect of the $150,000 engineering building for the University of Michigan and the other, perhaps even more significant, came from a lady client who wanted him to design an apartment block, The Palms. Kahn made the bold decision to build the Palms Apartments from reinforced concrete. Michigan was a heavy producer of Portland cement, as it had rich marl deposits in at least a dozen areas, several of them in the south east of the state where many of the motor manufacturers were located. The use of reinforced concrete for buildings was still a sufficiently new art for Albert Kahn, when asked by his younger brother Julius 'How do you calculate the strength of the reinforced concrete?' to reply: 'By guess—there are no scientific data'. Julius, who had graduated as an engineer, was horrified: he designed a type of carefully calculated reinforcement in which the strength of steel filling in concrete structural members could be precisely determined. This type of reinforcement was christened the Kahn Bar in his honour. The Kahn brothers organised the Truscon Company to produce these special reinforcing bars and the system was employed by the US Army to build its new war college.

Another who heard of the Kahns' success in building with reinforced concrete was Henry Bourne Joy, who had recently taken over Packard. Joy and his fellow stockholders decided to erect a new purpose built factory for the production of Packard cars, and put up $250,000 to erect a new and modern factory designed by Kahn on a 40 acre farm—outside Detroit's city limits. The design of the Packard factory aroused much scepticism, for it was a brick-faced structure built in reinforced concrete with generous window areas. It had 'arched and awninged windows in the front, and side and back windows so closely spaced that the walls seemed to be almost solid sheets of glass'. The secret of the new design was the metal sash windows developed by Julius Kahn which were first used in the Packard factory.

In 1908 Henry Ford, who had already outgrown two factories (his first plant at Mack Avenue, Detroit, is preserved in scaled down form in the Henry Ford

The assembly hall of the Daimler factory in Cannstatt in 1900. Somewhere in this apparent confusion the first Mercedes car is taking shape. This wooden structure was totally destroyed by fire on the eve of the 1903 Gordon Bennett Race, with the result that a 60 hp car, borrowed from a private owner, won the race, the works cars of 90 hp having been incinerated.

museum at Greenfield Village) commissioned Kahn to design what would be the largest factory in Michigan. Ford had bought a former race track north of Detroit for the plant site, which ran for a fifth of a mile on Woodward Avenue and was to contain six acres of floor space. Ford had told his partner, James Couzens, that he would like the entire field covered with one roof; Couzens gave this brief to Kahn, who not only designed the plant under one roof but designed it to accommodate future expansion with ease. It was the first of more than a thousand buildings for Ford to be designed by Kahn. He was also responsible for Ford's huge Rouge plant, which is still the hub of Ford production in the United States.

However, this first commission for Ford, which became known as Highland Park, was perhaps the most significant, for it was in this 'crystal palace' that Ford first applied the principles of mass production to the building of motor cars in 1913. Though the Highland Park plant still exists today, its manufacturing days are over and it is now used for storage purposes.

Before his death in 1942, Kahn had designed factories for Chrysler and General Motors as well as Ford and Packard. He designed over 150 factories and a headquarters building for GM. Kahn, praised by the American Institute of Architects as 'master of concrete and steel, master of space and time', summed up his philosophy of factory building in a speech to an American arts and crafts society meeting: 'There is no reason why utility and beauty cannot go together. In fact, pure beauty is only to be found in the highest utility. Beauty is natural. Modern industry has proved that it costs no more to plan a building that provides for the welfare of the workmen. The old factory, erected without thought of its purpose—to house living beings who were creating things—was ugly because it was built without purpose. Utility, efficiency and beauty are handmaidens'. Certainly, Kahn's principles were widely followed by other

Above *A Model T Ford chassis under test at Highland Park, Detroit, in 1914. Ford's 'Crystal Palace', designed by Albert Kahn, was the first car factory to incorporate a moving production line.*
Below *Henry Ford promised all his 1914-15 customers a rebate if his company's profits exceeded a certain level. This $50 cheque was one of hundreds of thousands duly paid out.*

factory architects. When Ford decided to build a new European factory at Dagenham in the mid 1920s, it was built very much on the lines that Kahn had laid down, even though the architect was an Englishman, Major C.R. Heathcote. He was to die in his 40s before the Dagenham plant was completed. And when Ford decided to build a factory in Stockholm, Sweden, they employed a local architect called Uno Ahren. This building, opened in 1930 in Stockholm, closely followed the pattern laid down at other Ford locations.

Albert Kahn also designed a number of private houses of distinction. Once a year he would take commissions to build a private house, usually executed at a loss as his company had become so geared to mass producing factory designs. He usually designed these buildings in Tudor or Georgian idioms, far removed for his normal work, but perhaps his favourite from among all these 'Albert's

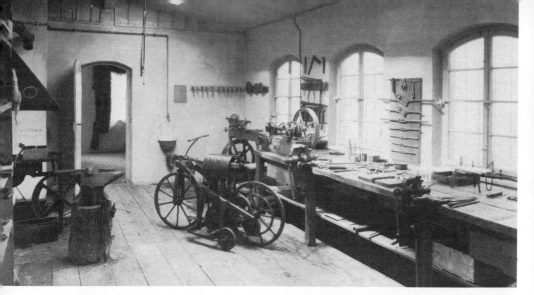

The workshop in Bad Cannstatt, where Gottlieb Daimler built his first engines, in its original state. A restored replica of this workshop was opened in 1964.

babies' was the house he built for Edsel Ford, basically a reinforced concrete structure, but clad in Briar Hill sandstone to resemble an English Cotswold house.

In 1944 a Dodge truck factory which Kahn had designed in 1938 was selected by the New York Museum of Modern Art as an outstanding example of American architecture in the previous 12 years. The judges commented: 'The factory has advanced to become one of our most distinguished categories. This plant reflects design to serve the purpose well: windowed walls and roof monitors, where much natural light is needed; organisation of the unit so that production steps are taken in orderly progress, forming proud and useful architecture'.

Probably the oldest European factory incorporating Kahn's principles is the Ford plant in Cork, Ireland. Work on this plant started in 1917; it was to provide tractors for Britain to beach the German blockade of allied shipping during the Great War. It went into production in 1919 but fall in demand for tractors post-war caused it to become an assembly plant three years later, providing Model T's for Ireland, and *via* its foundry, cylinder blocks for the Ford factory at Trafford Park, Manchester. Externally much as it was when it opened on the frontage facing the River Lee in Cork's Marina, the factory is still very active today, assembling Ford Cortinas for the Irish market, which it has dominated since 1922.

In Auburn, Indiana, the old Auburn factory, a magnificent example of industrial Art Deco architecture, has been revived, and now houses examples not only of the products of the Auburn-Cord-Duesenberg group but also locally-produced marques from Albany to Zimmerman (both gawky high-wheeled motor buggies) as well as special-interest cars like Lincoln Continental V12, Model T Ford Speedster, Chrysler Imperial and Rolls-Royce Phantom I.

Would-be hunters of old-time car factories will find *The World's Automobiles* by the late G.R. Doyle (Temple Press) a valuable aid. Last published in the early 1960s, *The World's Automobiles* is an alphabetical listing of car makers, with the addresses of their plants.

One of the most famous car factories, the Bugatti works in Molsheim, Alsace, still stands intact, with the house and outbuildings adjoining from which Ettore Bugatti conducted his business in 'feudalismo' fashion.

The car plants of Paris

Up to the mid-1970s, the automotive past of Paris was still there for all to see. Mostly untouched by wartime bombing, the old buildings just found new uses once their car-making days had ended. But the flurry of new building in the Paris suburbs has changed all that. Where the stark towers of La Defense now rear beyond the Porte Maillot was once the centre of the more *artisanal* side of the French car industry, whole streets of little garages busy turning out light cars and cyclecars from proprietory components, new establishments budding off like polyps as the foreman of the enterprise, convinced he could do as well—if not better than Renault or Citroën—broke away to set up on his own. But if that aspect of the colourful past of the Parisian car industry has vanished, and if a garish block of flats now rises on the site of the old Salmson factory on the Quai du Point du Jour at Boulogne-sur-Seine, much still survives, and Levallois is still the place, notes Jacques Potherat, where you can find the workshops of bargain-price mechanics!

The great Citroën factory on the old Quai du Javel (now Quai André Citroën) and the just pre-Second World War Ford works at Poissy (now occupied by Chrysler-France) may be nowadays regarded just as typical car factories (though their design was truly advanced for their day), but Louis Renault's works at Boulogne-Billancourt, reconstructed after wartime bombing on May 5 1942, can still prove surprisingly impressive at first sight. For the core of the factory is built in the middle of the Seine, on the Ile Seguin, and breasts the waters like a great white *Transatlantique*, with a block of offices across its bow serving as a bridge. And hidden deep in the huge Renault complex is the little shed where Louis Renault built his first car in 1898, in the garden of his rich button-maker father's house. It is, however, largely a replica. There were no tools, no bench and no machinery surviving before the shed was reconstructed in the 1960s by Maurice Broual.

Past has a way of mingling with present in Paris: continue along the Seine on the Quai Nationale, and you come to a high red-brick building with 'Blériot-Aéronautique' picked out on its façade, which is now an Aérospatiale factory.

During the early 1920s the Blériot factory in Paris, faced with a fall in aircraft orders due to the outbreak of peace in 1918, built twin-cylinder cyclecars.

Though the aeronautical past of the Blériot factory is unquestionably more famous, during the immediate post-Great War period, when orders for new aeroplanes were non-existent, this factory produced Blériot cyclecars and motorcycles in large numbers.

A little further on, and you come to the old Georges Richard-Unic factory, later taken over by Fiat-France and partially demolished in mid-1979, though the surviving part still carries the Unic badge in mosaic roundels. Here Georges Richard, having broken with Brasier after that firm's great days when it won the Gordon Bennett Cup for France, produced solid, reliable cars—and many of London's taxis—before his firm became merely the truck-making wing of Simca.

Approaching Puteaux, you notice on the left an overgrown building occupied by a firm supplying house plants: this is the old De Dion Bouton factory, which went into a steady decline in the 1920s and ended up making motor scooters. Even in the 1940s, the octogenarian Marquis de Dion and his equally decrepit Abyssinian chauffeur Zélélé could be seen driving round Paris, in a De Dion of venerable aspect! In May 1980, the Quai Nationale was renamed 'Quai De Dion Bouton' in honour of its most famous car factory.

Turn left into Courbevoie, and you see on your right in a very short distance a little garage in a yard: on the door to the adjoining house is a neatly-engraved brass plate inscribed 'A. Marguerite'. It was here that M Marguerite built sporty little cyclecars in the 1920s, including one of the oddest examples of badge engineering ever recorded. The rich protector of music hall star Cora Madou ordered a series of cars from Marguerite bearing her name as a present for his mistress . . ..

Follow the Boulevard de Verdun; you will come to a Berliet warehouse on the left. This was part of the Delage works. Nearby in the Rue Jules Ferry, is the remains of the Darmont works, which built Morgan three-wheelers under licence. A couple of kilometres down the road is Bois-Colombes. There, the flying stork emblem of Hispano Suiza still decorates the Hispano factory's wind tunnel—they moved into aviation after they abandoned cars—and is emblazoned across the factory frontage. Hispano adopted the stork in homage to the consumptive First World War flying ace Georges Guynemer, whose SPAD was powered by an Hispano V8 aero engine. He flew with the famous Escadrille de Cigognes—the 'Stork Squadron'—and the Hispano stork was taken from the emblem painted on the fuselage of his biplane. You can see the development of the Escadrille Cigogne stork insignia in the special display at the Musée de l'Air at Meudon, southwest of Paris. (Another marque using the flying stork emblem was Bignan-Sport.)

Guynemer himself did not drive an Hispano (though an equally famous fighter ace who subsequently brought out his own make of luxury car, Réné Fonck, *did* own an Alfonso XIII Hispano) but drove a humbler car, a Sigma. His car is preserved today in the museum at Compiègne, and Guynemer's statue stands at the end of one of the town's main thoroughfares. In 1919 Sigma brought out a sporting model called the type Guynemer, which sold for Fr 13,000. The Sigma factory was destroyed in 1968. Not far away in the Rue Armand Sylvestre, Courbevoie, is the factory of La Licorne, an impressive white four-storey building, surprisingly large for a firm whose renown was almost entirely confined to its country of origin but which surprisingly survived from 1901 to 1950.

Cross the bridge into Levallois, and on the left is a long grey factory occupying two blocks. This is the former Clément-Bayard works, and bisected by the Rue Clément-Bayard, recalling that astute businessman Adolphe Clément, who sold the rights to his name along with the popular Clément marque, changed his name to Clément-Bayard after a statue of the legendary 'chevalier sans peur et sans reproche' which stood outside his factory at

Below left *A surviving Paris 'octroi' building. The octroi was the bane of motorists until the abandonment, on New Year's day, 1930, of a tax on petrol in the tanks of cars entering the French capital. The octroi dated back to the days when Paris was a walled city. Motorists driving out of Paris were issued with green vouchers recording the amount of petrol in their tanks; any excess on their return to the city was subject to the local petrol tax. Food was also taxed at the octroi stations.*

Below right *Opened at the turn of the century, Adolphe Clément's former factory at Levallois-Perret still carries his monogram, though today it builds Citroën 2 cv cars.*

Mezières and went on to produce cars, airships and huge aero engines under the new marque name. Keep going past the Clément-Bayard factory, and on the right you soon come to an amazing survival from the 1920s, the Garage Sirejols. It claimed to sell BNC cars, though that marque expired in the early 1930s, carrying BNC enamel signs inside and out till 1980. In its dusty interior—it is simply a lock-up nowadays—is a *'très de l'époque'* mural of motor racing. M Sirejol's name is still on the office door though he died several years ago. Nearby is the workshop in the Rue Raspail where Ruby proprietory engines— mainstay of many French light cars in the 1920s and 1930s—were manufactured, while on the Ile de la Grande Jatte the building occupied in the 1920s by the French agent for Rudge Whitworth wheels still carries the painted legend 'Roues Rudge Whitworth'.

Motor showrooms

In the very early days, it was common practice for the purchaser of a new motor car to collect it—either in person or by proxy in the shape of a 'motor servant'— from the factory that had built it. It was, after all, a vehicle which in most cases had been custom built to his specification and bodied with the same degree of personal attention from the *carrossier* as the owner would have expected had he been buying a Savile Row suit or a pair of Purdey shotguns. Garages for service and storage of motor cars were already in existence by the turn of the century (by that time, Bordeaux already had ten of them, the world's first service station having been opened in that city at 41, rue St Claire in 1895) but it was not long before motor agents, especially for the more fashionable makes, began to open splendid showrooms to display their wares to prospective customers.

One of the finest was that opened by the Parisian Mercedes agent 'C.L. Charley' (his real name was Charles Lehmann) in the Champs Elysées. The ornate 'Mercedes-Palace' was at number 70, a typically Parisian building laid out to show the vehicles on display at their best, with a viewing gallery running the length of the showroom on either side. One of the first big commercial garages in London was opened in 1902 behind S.F. Edge's Motor Power Company, at 14, New Burlington Street. The garage, which held 50 cars on

three floors, with access by lift, was reached through the archway alongside the famous wine merchants, Hedges & Butler (whose then proprietor, Frank Hedges Butler, was a pioneer motorist and balloonist). This was not, however, London's first multi-storey garage. That had been opened in May 1901 by the City & Suburban Electric Carriage Company at 6, Denman Street, near Piccadilly Circus. It had seven floors, linked by a three-ton electric lift, and a floor area of 19,000 square feet.

Changing fashions have meant that most early motor car showrooms have been swept away or incorporated in later buildings; however, one magnificent survivor is the Automobile Palace opened in the Welsh spa town of Llandindrod Wells, Radnorshire, around 1910 by the cycle and motor agent, Tom Norton.

Above left *Up to 1979 the Garage Siréjols in Levallois-Perret carried enamel BNC advertisements on its walls; but when this photograph was taken in the spring of 1980 most of the signs had been removed.*

Above *This was what a typical petrol station of the 1920s looked like, before the 'corporate identity' departments of the oil companies were set up to tidy the appearance of their agencies. On the forecourt of this Chiswick garage is a 1926 Clyno tourer.*

Right *Still extant in the Belgian town of Ghent is this magnificent Ford agency of the 1920s, complete with 'Ford', 'Fordson' and 'Lincoln' lettered in stained glass on its ground-floor windows.*

Norton, a local character who had been in the motor trade since 1899, went so far as to advertise on his building that he was also a supplier of aircraft, though one imagines that the undulating Radnorshire terrain was not particularly suitable for experiments with stick and string aeroplanes. The Automobile Palace is still one of the features of the town, and has on display a remarkable collection of early bicycles.

Another motor showroom dating from around the same time is that of Rolls-Royce Motors in London's Conduit Street, in the heart of the fashionable West End, and originally used to display Mors and Panhard cars which C.S. Rolls sold before he met Royce. This showroom is still very much in use by Rolls-Royce, and for many years had on display the famous 1906 40/50 hp six-cylinder AX 201, the original 'Silver Ghost'. The Rolls-Royce showroom is unusual in surviving in a busy city, where all too often showrooms are swept away by the hand of the moderniser and the developer. Typically, the original Morris garage, founded by William Morris in Longwall Street, Oxford, before he turned to car manufacturing in 1912, was demolished in 1979, to make way for extensions to Nuffield College, and only the façade was preserved. And Ford's garage at No 8 Balderton Street, London, W1, stands on the site of London's first garage, opened by the Motor Supply Company in June 1900.

It is more common to find old-time showrooms in the smaller provincial towns, where there is less pressure to change one's image to keep up with fashion. Near Brentwood in Essex, for instance, there is still a motor agency with a 1930s advertisement for John Bull tyres on display, a Rolls-Royce Phantom II chassis waiting to be rebuilt on the same spot which it has occupied for the past decade and, until recently, the remains of a 1920s bus body rotting in the undergrowth outside.

One feature of old garages which has almost totally vanished is the hand-wound petrol pump, which has been rendered extinct by escalating petrol prices and proposals to sell petrol in Britain in litres, as is the practice in Europe. In the early 1970s it was still possible to find rural wayside garages which dispensed petrol from hand pumps, but nowadays, even where petrol pumps of this kind are retained, it is only as a display item. Incidentally, there is a remarkable collection of early petrol pumps on show at the Donington Race Circuit, which, founded in the 1930s, fell into disrepair after the war. It has been totally rebuilt during the 1970s by Leicester builder, Tom Wheatcroft, who used to visit the old track as a boy before the war. Though some of the old buildings remain, Donington can hardly be counted as a preserved track, for it has had to be totally rebuilt and in some cases rerouted to comply with modern regulations.

The simplest way of locating early garages is to read the advertisement pages of pre-war magazines and actually go and see whether a building listed at a given address still exists or whether it has been rebuilt; it is possible, in some out of the way garages, to come across early literature or photographs which have been put on one side over the years. Former coachbuilders' premises can also be rewarding; around 1965, coming back through Canterbury, I happened to pass the premises of the well known coachbuilders, Bligh Brothers, which had built the bodywork for Count Louis Zborowski's Chitty-Chitty-Bang-Bangs. The place was in the process of being gutted and much of its contents had already been destroyed, though I was able to save some early motoring magazines from the bonfire.

Racing circuits

Although motor racing had begun as early as 1895, the construction of special tracks for speed events did not begin until the turn of the century. This was mainly due to the fact that while, on the continent, motorists were permitted—and even encouraged—to race on the public highway, in Britain the law forbade speeds in excess of 12 mph and any form of motor sport was frowned on by the authorities, though hill-climbs were organised on the highway at Dashwood Hill (Buckinghamshre), Tilburstowe Hill (Godstone, Surrey) and Westerham Hill (Kent). Only on private ground could motorists reach high speeds with impunity: the private drive on the Duke of Portland's estate at Clipstone was long enough for Charles Jarrott, on a 70 hp Panhard, to achieve a world record speed of 79.3 mph (127 km/h) in August 1902 over a flying kilometre.

It was the wealthy landowner Earl De la Warr who instituted the first automobile speed course on his private estate at Bexhill-on-Sea in Sussex. The De la Warr Parade along the sea front had originally been developed by the Earl as a cycle track, and was resurfaced and extended to a kilometre in length to accommodate automobile speed trials. Because the Parade was on the Earl's private land, it was not subject to any speed restrictions, and the Sussex police, who were particularly severe in their enforcement of the 12 mph limit, were powerless to prevent speed trials there. The Parade was bounded at one end by Galley Hill, a slight gradient which enabled competitors to gather momentum on their way across the starting line, while a half mile extension at the westward end gave ample space for braking.

The events held at Bexhill were purely aimed at determining maximum speed over the flying kilometre, and the opening event, staged on Whit Monday 1902, saw an entry list of over 200 vehicles, fastests of which was a Serpollet steam car *Oeuf de Pâques* ('Easter Egg') which achieved an average of 54.5 mph along the course. Races were held on the Parade until 1925, in which year there was a general ban on motor racing competitions on the highway in Britain following an accident to an ex-Raymond Mays Brescia Bugatti driven by one F. Giveen in a hill-climb at Kop Hill near Princes Risborough in Buckinghamshire. Today, Marine Parade at Bexhill reveals nothing of its historic motoring past, though Madiera Drive at nearby Brighton, opened in 1905 for automobile speed trials,

A timeless picture of the Brighton Speed Trials on Madeira Drive. This Alfa-Mercedes duel was photographed in the late 1950s.

is still the scene of two historic motoring events; each November it is the finish of the annual London-Brighton Veteran Car Run, while each September the Brighton and Hove Motor Club organises speed trials on the Drive. Attracting all types of car, these events are among the oldest established motor sport events in the world.

British enthusiasts, however, did not remain satisfied with sprint events run off against the clock. A speed hill-climb course at Shelsley Walsh, in the Midlands, was inaugurated by the Midlands Automobile Club in 1905 and is still active today, providing greater excitement than a sheer straight line course (and incidentally breeding a whole race of 'Shelsley Specials'), but the motoring enthusiasts really wanted to see cars racing one another on a circuit rather than purely attempting to beat the clock. In 1967 I met Mr L.F. Anstead, who then owned a little garage behind the Ship Hotel in Weybridge, Surrey, who was able to tell me exactly what brought Brooklands, the world's first purpose built race circuit, into being.

'In September 1905 Hugh Fortesque Locke King went to Brescia, in Italy, to see the race for the Florio Cup, in his 60 hp Itala, of which make he was an enthusiastic owner. The British branch of the Itala company had their factory on his estate at Weybridge, among farmhouses and pinewoods.

'I started work at the Itala factory in 1914 for the princely salary of half-a-crown a week. Locke King had no financial interest in the company as is sometimes supposed.

'My father-in-law was Locke King's chauffeur, and drove all his Italas. The Manager of the Itala company when I joined was the racing driver, Foresti, (who is said to have taken the 120 hp Itala which won the 1907 Brescia Cup round the track at 110.2 mph on test) while Robertson Shersby-Harvie, who drove for the company, used to test Dunlop tyres on the racing Italas.

'Anyway, Locke King never did manage to see the Coppa Florio, because his car collided with the cliff wall on an Italian mountain road, damaging the

A 1934 Ford V8-40 with English tourer coachwork starting at Shelsley Walsh sometime in the late 1930s. This photograph was printed from a glass-plate negative, one of several hundred discovered by the author dumped in a former paint store at a Ford plant (Ford Archives).

A line-up of famous Brooklands racing cars by the memorial to the former race circuit at a 1967 rally which commemorated the 60th anniversary of the track's opening.

steering. The crippled Itala limped into Brescia on the evening of September 10, to find the race over and the inn full of the talk of the victory which Raggio, an amateur, driving his first major race, had won in his 112 hp Itala, followed by Duray's De Diétrich, Lancia's FIAT and Hemery's Darracq.

'Not one Englishman or English make of car had entered.

'On his return home, Locke King became more and more convinced that what Britain needed was a closed racing circuit designed for high speed competition', Mr Anstead concluded.

So Locke King called a meeting of noted motorists, S.F. Edge and Charles Jarrott among them. Suggestions were made as to the form the track should take; it was decided that the banked curves should be concave, not convex like a cycle track or *vélodrome*. Nothing of the kind had ever been attempted before. The man chosen to draw up the plans was Colonel Charles Capel Holden, RE, former chairman of the Royal Automobile Club. The Brooklands Track (so-called after Locke King's house which looked down on it from the far side of the railway line), was to be a huge concrete amphitheatre, with a hundred-foot-wide track almost three miles round on which cars would run without steering effort at speeds of 120 mph, carried round the almost 30-foot-high banked curves by centrifugal force. The site on which the great motor track was to be built was low lying marshy meadowland, where the River Wey meandered below the pine trees of St George's Hill. A few farmhouses, including Foxlake Farm, Byfleet, which Locke King had to purchase to accommodate the Byfleet Banking's curve, were dotted over the area.

In the autumn of 1906, all the contracts were signed, and an army of labourers moved in to start the work of construction. The main contractors were Price & Reeves of Weybridge, who recruited between 1,500 and 2,000 Irishmen, who brought 'wives, children and hangers-on', and established a shanty town of 18 or 20 huts built of tree branches, ferns and corrugated iron, devoid of sanitation or proper water supply. Seven miles of railway track were laid down, linked to the London and South Western line, and six locomotives dealt with the movement of ten steam cranes and a steam navvy, and the 80 truckloads of concrete which arrived each day. Despite their squalid living conditions, the labourers working on the track seem to have been cheerful enough, holding nightly sing-songs round their camp fires. Mrs Locke King (who later became Dame Ethel) came to these gatherings, questioning the men about their lot, with which it seemed they were largely satisfied.

Henry T. Castlemaine, whose father was landlord of The Plough Inn at Byfleet, recalled that while the labourers would cheerfully spend all their wages on getting fighting drunk on a Saturday night, nevertheless they were always ready to give the four-year-old Henry a joy-ride in the railway trucks on the site. For ten months the Irishmen laboured by day and caroused by night. Following complaints from the residents of Weybridge of the possibility of a smallpox epidemic, the shanty town was razed to the ground in April 1907, and a communal hut (more insanitary, if anything, than the shanties) erected. Due to the low lying situation of the track, serious flooding was sometimes experienced. However, work continued, bankings were built and trees demolished. The 2,000 Irishmen, using manpower, horsepower and steam power, laid 200,000 tons of concrete, mostly on a basis of sand, which unfortunately led to subsidence. A ferro-concrete bridge of deceptively frail appearance, subcontracted to the French Hennebique Company, carried the banking over the River Wey. It never subsided, thus causing the famous 'big bump', as the sand-based banking on either side sank slightly.

When the last labourer had left Brooklands in the summer of 1907, and the vast track lay painfully white in the hot June sun, journalists and motorists alike crowded to see it and marvel at its sheer size. The circuit was $2\frac{11}{16}$ miles round on the inner edge of the 100 foot wide track. Of this two miles were level, while at the Weybridge and Byfleet ends of the track were two huge concave bankings, round which the cars could hurtle as though on the end of a string. The shorter banking, at the Weybridge end was known as the Members' or Home Banking, and was struck on a 1,000 foot radius and the maximum height of the bank was 28 feet 8 inches. The Byfleet Banking, struck on a radius of 1,550 feet, was 21 feet 10 inches high at its maximum. The bankings were built up from earth

Racing at Brooklands had much in common with horse-racing: in the very early days, the drivers wore racing colours (these were subsequently transferred to the cars) and bookmakers offered odds on the races. Most famous of the Brooklands bookies (who are seen here in action along the enclosure railings on a mid-1920s afternoon) was a lugubrious character known as 'Long Tom'.

As the Brooklands track settled over the years, its surface became irregular. Here Kaye Don's Bugatti becomes airborne over the 'big bump' on the Members' Banking in the 1933 500 Miles Race.

and sand, and the concrete was poured straight on, using wooden formers to give the correct shape. When the track dropped down to the level from the Byfleet Banking, it negotiated a gentle reverse curve, passing round the Itala Works at a respectful distance, and then rose again into the Members' Banking, which ran through a cutting round the natural Members' Hill.

Halfway down this level stretch, there was a fork, opposite the Itala works, where the $\frac{5}{8}$ mile long Finishing Straight led off at an angle, past the Club House and the Paddock, rising to meet the Members' Banking in the approximate centre of its curve. Cars finishing in a race were expected to negotiate a fairly sharp curve at the end of this straight and run along the foot of the banking until they came to a road leading back to the Paddock. In order to help them, as speeds rose, a number of finishing lines was used. The slowest cars used the Long Finishing Line, about halfway down the Straight and faster cars finished progressively nearer the Fork. There was the Short Finishing Line, the Special Short Finishing Line and then the Lightning Finishing Line. Finally, speeds got so high that to use the Finishing Straight at all was a matter of some concern; cars could shoot out into the middle of the Members' Banking and collide with a slower competitor who was still lapping, or worse still, shoot over the top of the banking and fall on the other side. To avoid this, cars finished on the outer circuit.

A variety of starting lines was also used, in the Finishing Straight or on the level by the Fork (known as the Pond Start from the pond just behind the track) or down on the Long Straight by the railway. In fact, when all the various ways in which the track could be traversed were taken into account, the number of different circuits possible became almost infinite, especially when chicanes were introduced into some of the long distance races. A road-racing circuit known as the Campbell Circuit was opened in the track's 30th year, on April 20 1937, to add another element to the varied appeals of Brooklands.

The construction of the great oval track, with its two banked curves, its

Left *This lap counter and signal were used when Brooklands was first opened to indicate to drivers when to turn into the Finishing Straight at the end of a race.*

Below *Because local residents objected to night-time racing at Brooklands after S.F. Edge's 1907 24-hour record, the British equivalent of the Le Mans 24-hour race had to be held in 12-hour stints on two successive days. This is the 'Le Mans' start of the 1929 'Double-Twelve' race at Brooklands.*

Below right *Standing in front of the Brooklands Clubhouse in this mid-1920s photograph is Parry Thomas' 'Flat-Iron' Special, which had a 1.5 litre straight-eight engine of fiendish complexity.*

graded finishing straight designed to help cars to pull up before rejoining the main circuit, its clubhouse based on Locke King's Mena House Hotel (near the Pyramids in Egypt), its grandstands, its paddock and its tuning sheds, cost Locke King between £150,000—£250,000, a considerable sum for those days. Brooklands remained in use right up until the Second World War, though it was becoming increasingly unsuitable for high speed motor racing. As it had only been laid on sand foundations, the track surface had become extremely uneven and the cars travelling at over 100 mph often became airborne on the 'big bump' on the Byfleet Banking. An aerodrome had existed at Brooklands since 1909 and, during the Great War, Vickers had set up a large factory on the site of the Itala works. The aviation activities at Brooklands had become increasingly important (it was here that Barnes Wallis developed his famous Tallboy and Grand Slam bombs) and after the Second World War Vickers took over the track entirely and parts of the banking were demolished to enable aircraft to take off. During the 1960s, four-engined VC10 jet airliners were built at

Brooklands and flown out, in stripped form, to Vickers' aerodrome at nearby Wisley for final fitting out.

The old circuit therefore fell into disuse, and many of its historic features were demolished, though the club house, the first aircraft booking shed and other historic features have been carefully preserved and sufficient remained in the 1970s for some restoration work to be done by the Brooklands Society who hold an annual reunion at the track. There has been for many years talk of establishing some form of national transport museum at Brooklands, though this seems just as far from realisation today as it was when it was first mooted in the mid 1960s. There has also been talk of holding races for vintage cars on the old Campbell Circuit, the only part of the track which could be returned to its original use, though as Sir Malcolm Campbell was the man who decided on the closure and sale of the Brooklands Circuit, this would surely be the supreme irony!

Other banked circuits followed the Brooklands example, notably Indianapolis in America, opened in 1911 and still in use for the annual Indianapolis 500 Race. It studiously preserves one narrow strip of track paved with bricks, as originally the entire circuit was surfaced with brick, giving it its popular nickname of the 'Brickyard'.

In 1927 an autodrome was completed at San Martin, a suburb of Buenos Aires, Argentina, 12 miles from the city centre. The track, with a lap length of three kilometres, was a banked oval of concrete, and had three huge stands accommodating several thousand spectators alongside the finishing straight. The plans were to hold race meetings every weekend, mainly restricted to standard cars and sports models, as there were very few actual racing cars in Argentina. Banked circuits of the 1920s which still survive include Sitges, in Spain, (where the Catalan old car club holds an annual rally) and Miramas in France's Camargue region. But only one circuit remains where you can still see historic cars in action on a banked track. That is Montlhéry, some 15 miles south of Paris, where the Linas-Montlhéry circuit opened in 1924; it is taken over every year for the Coupes de l'Age d'Or, open to vintage and classic racing cars.

Montlhéry Circuit, opened for racing in October 1924, was the brainchild of one Monsieur Lamblin, who ran a magazine entitled *L'Aérosport* and owned a

radiator manufacturing company. He bought a 12,000 acre estate to the west of the Paris-Orléans road and commissioned the civil engineer Raymond Jamin to create the fastest motor racing track in the world. The basic circuit, 2,584 metres in length, consisted of two steeply banked curves linked by short straights, though leading from the finishing straight was a road circuit incorporating all types of bend so that a complete lap of the entire autodrome was 12.5 km. Various combinations of the banked and level track could be used, creating eight distinct circuits.

Today, Montlhéry has a period atmosphere which cannot be equalled by any other race circuit. It still has the old lock-up garages incorporated in the ferro-concrete structure of the main banking, while there are none of the ugly metal crash barriers which make modern race circuits so unattractive. Instead, there is a wide grass strip on the inside of the track which ends in an earth banking above which the spectators stand behind concrete fencing. Watching powerful classic cars racing on the Montlhéry banking has an excitement totally absent from today's 'Mickey Mouse' Grand Prix circuits and their low-built cars in which all that can be seen of the driver is the top of his helmet. At Montlhéry the angle of the banking is such that you can actually look almost directly into the cockpit as the driver passes you and see every movement of the wheel. To control speed at the track, a number of artificial chicanes has been incorporated into the banked section, and these make for exciting racing as the entire pack of cars jockeys for the best position in and out of the bend.

Even the concrete ticket booths at Montlhéry are *'très de l'époque'*, and the atmosphere of the occasion is heightened by the fact that French enthusiasts all turn up at the event in period cars, those in open tourers naturally using these as a grandstand to view the proceedings. It is also interesting to note that the approach road to the track—it climbs a steep hill, and used to be used as a testing ground for Citroën cars—is named the Avenue Georges Boillot, after the cocky Frenchman who achieved so many sporting successes for Peugeot immediately before the Great War and who was shot down in aerial combat over the Western Front in 1915.

At Pont-de-Gennes, on the N23, about 20 kilometres east of Le Mans, ornate iron railings beside the road mark the twin tunnels (now derelict) that linked grandstands to 'replenishment depots' in the 1906 French Grand Prix, first race to bear the name.

Berlin's Avus track, opened in 1921 by the industrialist Hugo Stinnes, actually made use of the world's first motorway, originally planned in 1909, and almost completed when the Great War broke out. Its instigator, Karl Friedrich Fritsch, had planned the 6¼ mile 'autobahn' as a race and test track, linking its dual carriageways with a loop at either end. The Avus track is still used as a public highway, though its racing days are long past.

Race tracks that never were

I used to live within sight of what might have been the world's first purpose built motor track, had sufficient funds and enthusiasm been forthcoming shortly after the turn of the century. This was an ambitious proposal to build a huge race course on Riddlesdown, near Warlingham in Surrey, which came to nothing. However, there is a permanent reminder of another early track which never came into existence at Jaywick Sands, on the Essex coast. In 1900, a group of developers bought 428 acres of the Alton Park Estate at Clacton for £80,000 proposing to create a 'recreational suburb' with a golf course, polo field, sports ground, tennis courts, and croquet and bowls lawns. To be served by a proposed extension of the Great Eastern Railway, the development was to have incorporated a 2.5 mile oval motor race track. The track would have consisted of two mile straights linked by curved bankings, but the necessary finance, around £150,000, could not be raised and the scheme was abandoned. It seems that at some stage during the proceedings, the site was surveyed by Col H.C.L. Holden, who shortly afterwards was to design Brooklands; and by coincidence it was the name Brooklands that was later chosen to designate the estate developed on part of the site of the proposed race track by a Mr Stedman, who began work in 1928. Perhaps in deference to the motoring associations of the site, all its roads were named after makes of car popular in the late 1920s.

You enter the Brooklands estate, which can only be described as Essex shackery, past a towering building housing a go-cart track, and driving down Brooklands, which runs behind the sea wall, you come first to Swift Avenue then to Talbot Avenue and Wolseley Avenue; following that are Sunbeam, Hillman, Morris and Bentley Avenues which lead to the centre of the first phase of Brooklands, Brooklands Gardens, laid out in a square with the local shops and residents' association buildings around the perimeter. Continuing from Brooklands Gardens you come upon Austin, Alvis, Humber, Riley, Essex, Vauxhall, Fiat and Lancia Avenues, and then, driving down an awkwardly angled ramp which crosses the line of the old sea wall you drive into a muddy road called Midway from which lead Lincoln, Napier, Buick, Lanchester, Daimler, Standard, Rover, Singer, Crossley and Triumph Avenues before Midway peters out in a large puddle in the middle of the field. The Brooklands estate is scarcely picturesque, but it is unique: the only estate with so many car names.

A curious track survives at South Croydon in Surrey; it is clearly visible from the Brighton line train and can be glimpsed from the road, though it is now an industrial estate. It looks like a very complicated road racing circuit; in fact, the Autodrome was an ambitious driving school opened in 1936 by the local motor agent, Hubert Dees, to give learner drivers the opportunity to acquire road skills

Bentley Avenue and Wolseley Avenue, two of the roads named after cars on the Brooklands Estate at Jaywick Sands, Essex.

without venturing onto the public highway. This was because driving tests had just been introduced and represented a very great stumbling block to many would-be motorists. The Vintage Sports Car Club, which had been formed a little while before to preserve vehicles of the 1920s, lost little time in realising that here was an ideal venue for competition and held a speed trial at the Autodrome in 1937. However, the Autodrome seems to have been a concept too advanced for its time.

Other would-be race circuits never reached fruition. In January 1927 *The Autocar* carried news of an ambitious race track which was to be built under the auspices of the Brighton and Hove Motor Racing Club on the Sussex downs behind Brighton. Laid out in the shape of a flattened figure of eight, the track contained two separate circuits, which could be combined to give a total length of about six miles. The scheme included a test hill, a flying ground and a ground for motor cycle football. Among the directors of the scheme were the racing drivers Kenelm Lee Guinness (whose KLG spark plug factory, where the Irving-Napier land speed record car *Golden Arrow* was built in 1929 still stands on Putney Hill) and H.O.D. Segrave (who drove the *Golden Arrow* in its successful record attempt). Seven years later almost to the day, *The Autocar* noted that 'slowly the necessary preliminaries before the establishment of the Brighton Race Track are being completed . . ..' But the mid 1930s were a far less favourable climate for establishing a motor racing circuit than the late 1920s and the ambitious scheme came to nothing.

It was not the only scheme of its kind to be mooted. Similarly grandiose proposals were made to build a race track on the banks of the Wash in Lincolnshire around the same time by a consortium, which again included prominent racing drivers on the committee; again the proposals appeared in the press over a long period of time but once more the scheme turned out to be unrealistic. One of the great centres of the motoring social scene in the 1920s was Ardenrun House, the property of Captain Woolf Barnato, the wealthy diamond broker who financed the Bentley Company. It was here that he held parties for the smart set, and it was after one of these riotous events that the house eventually burnt down, leaving only the stableblock standing. However, the long drive of Ardenrun can still be seen on a by-road at Blindley Heath in Surrey; it was on this drive that the Bentley boys held impromptu races as part of Barnato's parties; it must have been a hair-raising feat for the drive is not particularly wide. I have in my possession the estate agent's catalogue used by Barnato when he went to view Ardenrun for the first time. A comprehensive and well illustrated document, the catalogue recalls a vanished era in motoring, in the days when motor racing was the prerogative of wealthy young men, who raced for fun, rather than paid professional drivers.

Michelin House

Perhaps the most amazing architectural monument to the golden age of motoring stands in London's Fulham Road. Michelin House, designed and built in 1909-10, is a unique piece of architecture. It has been described as a 'London building that deserves to survive on account of its bizarre character, the vitality and charm of its pictorial ceramic panels and the fact that it stands in time between Art Nouveau and the Motor Age'. Certainly it caused a sensation at the time of its opening, in January 1911, when the motor press noted that: 'A tour of inspection leaves an impression of a vast business, splendidly organised and

The exotic exterior of Michelin House in London's Fulham Road.

excellently housed.' The exuberance of the building reflects that fact that Michelin were at that time striving to assert themselves on the British market, in the face of opposition from the Du Cros interests who backed not only Dunlop tyres but also Napier and Gladiator cars.

Surprisingly, virtually nothing is known of Michelin House's architect, François Espinasse (1880-1925), who joined Michelin at Clermont-Ferrand in 1906 as an engineer ('construction de batiments et chef de chantier'). Espinasse designed Michelin's Paris headquarters at 97, boulevard Pereire in 1908 and was then given the commission of designing the company's new London office to replace their existing premises in two adjoining houses in Sussex Close (now part of the Old Brompton Road). It seems likely that Espinasse designed Michelin House under the close supervision of the Michelin brothers André (1853-1931) and Edouard (1859-1940).

The Michelin Company owed its foundation to the revolution of 1830 which overthrew King Charles X in favour of Louis Phillipe. The revolution left M Barbier, lawyer to the royal family, out of a job. He emigrated to Guadeloupe where he worked in a sugar factory. He later returned to France and set up in partnership with his cousin Edouard Daubrée of Clermont-Ferrand, a former captain in the King's light horse who had resigned his commission in 1830. Barbier and Daubrée established a sugar factory on the banks of the river Allier, but this was destroyed by floods and they returned to Clermont to set up a factory making agricultural machinery. Daubrée's mother ran a school for young ladies, which had a number of British pupils, and Daubrée fell in love with and married one of these, Elizabeth Pugh Barker. Miss Pugh Barker was the niece of the Scottish chemist, Mackintosh, who had discovered the method of waterproofing cloth by applying a solution of rubber dissolved in benzine and thus created the garment that bore his name.

Mackintosh also made rubber balls as playthings for his niece and Madame Daubrée, remembering the enjoyment she had had from these toys as a child, asked her husband to give her an unused corner of the factory in which she could experiment with their manufacture, with the help of a number of women workers. 'Her initiative was crowned with success as brilliant as it was lucrative, and the Daubrée factory became a very prosperous concern for the making of elastic balls'. The factory eventually concentrated entirely on rubber products; as early as 1833 Barbier had suggested covering the wheels of light carriages with rubber to lessen the road shocks. His daughter Adèle married Jules Michelin, and their sons had both achieved a measure of success as artists before they returned to take charge of the family business which was, at that period, experiencing a number of difficulties.

Edouard was a painter, and exhibited in the Salon of 1885, while André had spent a short time in the architectural department of the Beaux Arts (he left because his fellow students smoked too much and he could not stand the smell of their pipes). He then entered the Ministry of the Interior where he became Deputy Manager of the Cartographical department. He left in 1883 to set up in business on his own account as a locksmith and carpenter in Paris, but soon joined his brother at Clermont-Ferrand.

A fortuitous accident drew the brothers into the field of pneumatic tyres. In 1891 they were already making solid tyres for bicycles, when a cyclist arrived at their factory with one of the first pneumatic tyred cycles. This had punctured, and the cyclist had brought it to the works on the back of an oxcart. The tyres were of an unusual pattern, with hollow air-filled segments of rubber forming a tyre, which was stuck to the rims. The punctures, apparently, took four hours and 'very clever workmanship' to repair. When the repairs were complete, Edouard Michelin tried the machine out of curiosity, only to have a further puncture. Nevertheless he was so impressed by the increase in riding comfort given by the air-filled tyres that he decided to develop a pneumatic tyre that would be simpler to repair than the clumsy example he had just seen. The original Michelin detachable tyre was held to the rim by a number of small nuts and bolts, which tended to rust and break off.

Building on their experience with detachable cycle tyres, the Michelins adapted a Peugeot car (which they called *L'Eclair*) to take pneumatic tyres in 1895 and ran in the Paris-Bordeaux race that year. Their machine had a large box on the back to take spare tyres which was just as well because between Paris and Bordeaux they burst 22 air tubes. However, on the return trip to Paris they finished ninth. Despite this somewhat inauspicious start, by 1896 half the entries in the Paris-Marseilles race were fitted with pneumatic tyres.

By 1905, the Michelin brothers decided that it was time for them to set up a British branch company, since there were some 32,000 cars on the roads of Britain by that time. Because of the rapid growth of their business, they bought the site bordered by Fulham Road, Sloane Avenue, Leader Street and Lucan Place on which construction of a 22,000 square feet three-storey building began in 1910. The building was designed to fulfil a number of functions: it was to provide a prestigious company headquarters and office building, it was to incorporate a touring office and enquiry counter where tyres and touring information were dispensed, and provide a storage area for tyres complete with loading and unloading facilities, a repair workshop and a garage for delivery vans. The basement, which extended under the pavement and formed one continuous space thanks to the use of reinforced concrete supports, was reached by a lift and concrete stairs, and could store 30,000 inner tubes and 25,000 covers at once, and contemporary press reports claimed that: 'If the covers alone were placed on top of one another they would form a column more than 19 times the height of St Pauls'.

The building was constructed by the firm of L.G. Mouchelle, British agents for the Hennebique ferro-concrete system (which was also, incidentally, used for the concrete bridge which carried the Brooklands motor track across the River Wey). Mouchelle, the former French Consul for Wales, had become the British Hennebique agent for 1898, and had carried out a number of important industrial contracts at the same time as the company was building Michelin House, also erecting the Liver building in Liverpool, a 17 storey building which was then Europe's tallest concrete structure. The first engineering drawings for Michelin House are dated 1910, and notice of intention to build was entered in the District Surveyors Account at Chelsea on March 17 1910.

The surveyor reported that the building was 'roofed-out' by December that year. A two storey extension was added to the building in 1922-24. The ferro-concrete construction of the building not only minimised fire risk (metal framed doors and windows were also used) but enabled the interior of the building to be laid out on an open plan basis. The building was entered from the road through one of three arches fronting onto the Fulham Road which gave access to an entrance hall (now a tyre fitting bay) from which a metal framed door led to the reception area. The door opened automatically when somebody trod on the mat. This was an exceptionally advanced feature for the time, and would obviously have been of great value to customers who entered carrying tyres.

The reception area, 35 feet by 36 ft 5 in had a full width wooden counter where customers' enquiries were answered, tyres were received for repair and new tyres were sold, these being brought from the stockroom in about a minute and a half. From the reception area, a door led to the touring office. The facilities offered in the touring office incuded large roll-up maps of Britain and western Europe, together with the famous Michelin touring guides which could be studied either at tables or in comfortable chairs. A member of staff was on hand to help motorists plan their routes. André Michelin had created a similar service in Paris in 1908, but the idea was totally new in Britain. Michelin had put his brief cartographical training to good use by undertaking the mapping of France, and had supplied local authorities with nameplates for towns and villages as well as pumice stone milestones with vitreous enamel signs fixed to them. Indeed, these Michelin signposts can still be seen in some parts of rural France.

The visitor to the building in 1911 would have been impressed, as is the present day observer, by the exterior decoration of Michelin House. This is virtually intact in its original form, though the yellow ceramic tyres which once topped the two corner towers on the Fulham Road frontage were removed a few years back and replaced by flagstaffs. The Fulham Road façade of the building is covered in brilliant white Burmantoft 'Marmo' tiles made by the Leeds Fireclay Company, an Edwardian development of terracotta cladding featuring a weather resistant and washable glazed surface. Offsetting the brilliance of these tiles are blue rusticated pedestals, inset horizontal blue green bands on the lower shafts of the columns and vertical shafts on the upper portion of the two central columns, with wide blue-green bands above the wrought iron grille spanning the entrance arches. Either side of the curved gable are yellow tyres crowning the pillars, a smaller version of the tyres which used to top the corner towers.

The first floor offices are marked by inset panels of blue-green terracotta tiles

PARIS-BORDEAUX
1895

1ᶜᴿᴱ VOITURE sur PNEUS MICHELIN

One of the ceramic tile designs in Michelin House.

below the windows, while the more utilitarian section of the building is treated in red and yellow brick. The crowning glory of Michelin House, however, is the series of 34 ceramic panels depicting early motor racing successes on Michelin tyres. There are eight panels in Sloane Avenue, four in Lucan Place and the rest are in the form of a frieze in the fitting bay and reception area. The earliest panel depicts the first success of the Michelin detachable bicycle tyre, by Charles Terront in the Paris-Brest Cycle Race of 1891; the most recent is the 1910 Coupe des Voiturette, while Michelin's interest in other sport is represented by Hubert Latham's Antoinette monoplane, which was covered with Michelin aeroplane sheeting. Shown in other panels are Bardon's De Dion tricycle in the 1897 Paris-Cabourg race, Levegh (pseudonym of one M Velghe) on a Mors in the 1900 Paris-Toulouse race, Girardot ('the eternal second') on a Panhard in the 1901 Gordon Bennett Cup, Guillaume on a Darracq in the 1902 Paris-Vienna, Lautenschlager on the Mercedes which won the 1908 French Grand Prix at Dieppe, Louis Renault on the Renault which took the light car prize in 1903 Paris-Madrid, Charron on his 1898 Paris-Amsterdam Panhard and Hémery on a Benz in the St Petersburg-Moscow race in 1908. The tiles, which were made by Gilardoni fils et cie, of 38, rue de Paradis, Paris, were almost certainly designed by—or at least inspired by—the work of Montaut and Gamy, the celebrated French lithographers. Unlike Montaut's normal work the pictures are framed in twirling Art Nouveau tendrils of oak leaves, presumably to symbolise victory. The centrepiece of the panelling, above the desk in the reception area shows King Edward VII and the Prince of Wales riding in a red Mercedes landaulette. The tiles framing this illustration are figures whose beards for no apparent reason are transformed into bluebells as they descend.

Opening Michelin House in January 1911, André Michelin referred to the 'late lamented King Edward VII, to a large extent responsible for the *entente cordiale* of which the Michelin Company was a tangible expression'. He was doubtless paying tribute to Edward's interest in motoring and preference for Michelin tyres, which had helped the firm establish itself in Britain, where in 1911 some 100,000 cars were registered. A vanished feature of Michelin House, possibly destroyed by wartime bombing, was a stained glass window depicting M Bibendum in his classic pose, with a raised champagne glass filled to the brim with nails and broken bottles, and the toast 'Nunc est Bibendum', signifying Michelin's advertised ability to 'drink the obstacle' in other words to swallow sharp objects without injury. The upper window in Lucan Place also showed Bibendum, this time riding a bicycle; the Sloane Avenue window is believed to have incorporated a stained glass Bibendum design, too. At night, these windows were illuminated by mercury vapour lamps which gave a ghostly, grey-blue light.

Incidentally, M Bibendum, today one of the best known company trade-marks, was originally devised by Edouard Michelin in 1898, who happened to notice a pile of tyres at an exhibition and noticed that if arms and legs were added, the pile would take on the shape of a man. Soon after, Michelin was shown a sketch of an enormous beer drinker raising his glass for the toast *'Nunc est Bibendum'* ('Now is the time for drinking') and he combined the two ideas to create the famous Michelin man, the first finished drawings of which were completed by the famous caricaturist O'Galop. The figure was christened M Bibendum after a famous racing driver, seeing André Michelin pass by, shouted 'There goes Bibendum'! O'Galop also designed a ceramic panel depicting Bibendum which was used as decoration on the corner of the Paris headquarters of the Michelin Company, which was later sold and converted into a restaurant. Today Michelin House still lives up to the contemporary comment of the *Automotor Journal* that: 'A very unusual form of architecture has been adopted that is well calculated to attract attention and constitute a permanent advertisement with all passers-by'.

Show buildings

Britain's first motor show took place in 1895, an open air display at Tunbridge Wells, Kent, organised by Sir David Salomons, a wealthy local landowner and proprietor of one of Britain's first fleets of motor cars. Salomons' home, Broomhill, is now a nursing home, and the pitiful remnants of some of the cars that took part in the display were unearthed locally a few years back, but were beyond restoration. The first indoor exhibition of cars in Britain was at the Stanley Cycle Show in the Agricultural Hall, Islington, on November 22-30 1895.

Other shows followed quickly: the first British show devoted entirely to cars took place at London's Imperial Institute on May 9 1896, attracting ten exhibitors, including Daimler, Humber, Arnold and Bersey. Later in 1896, Charles Cordingley, who ran the annual Laundry Exhibition in the Agricultural Hall, boosted falling attendance by putting on a display of motor cars. The Cordingley Show became an annual event, but was pushed out of existence by the shows organised from 1903 by the Society of Motor Manufacturers and Traders. When these started, there were four annual motor shows in

London—the National, the Stanley, Cordingley's and the SMMT, the latter being originally held in the Crystal Palace.

But in February 1905, the SMMT show moved to Olympia, the huge exhibition hall in Kensington which had previously been occupied by Barnum & Bailey's Circus, 'the greatest show on earth'. Now the 10,000 seats that had surrounded the circus rings had been cleared away, extra windows had been installed and the earth floor at Olympia had been concreted from end to end to create an exhibition area capable of taking motor manufacturers' show stands. The SMMT show stayed at Olympia until 1936, moving to Earls Court next year; Earls Court stayed the Show's home until 1978, when the Motor Show moved to the National Exhibition Centre near Birmingham.

France's first show was from December 11-25 1894 in the Palais de l'Industrie in the Champs Elysées. In the golden age of motoring, the Paris Salon took place in the art nouveau Grand Palais: it was here, in 1910, that the first public demonstration of neon lighting took place, the Salon being illuminated by two red neon tubes 35 metres long.

Monuments and memorials

Wherever you go in a country with a motoring past, it seems, you are likely to come across some memorial to great events of the past. In France, as mentioned elsewhere, there is the monument to Cugnot in Void; not very far away, at Bar-le-Duc, stands a memorial of a very different nature, yet equally significant in the history of the self-propelled vehicle. On a busy intersection is a plinth on which stands a very chubby—and very naked—cherub supporting a velocipede. For the pedal bicycle was invented at Bar-le-Duc in the 1860s by two brothers named Michaux. And it was the invention of the bicycle which made the first light motor cars possible, by bringing in engineering aimed at developing light, yet strong, structures. Hitherto, the rationale behind the design of self-propelled road vehicles had been that of the locomotive engineer, to build excesssively strong and excessively heavy. Of course, such vehicles earned an extremely bad reputation as destroyers of the road surface: the Michaux brothers changed all that. The Michaux monument was erected as the result of a subscription organised by the cycling paper *Le Vélo* in 1894.

France abounds in motoring memorials. In Paris, for instance, you can see the magnificent memorial to Emile Levassor at the Porte Maillot. Once a park on a busy main road, the garden in which the Levassor memorial stands is now isolated by the Boulevard Péripherique. Often the garden is full of children at play, but the last time I visited this memorial, the air was pierced by a lone cornettist, sitting above the pedestrian subway which runs beneath the gardens and playing a serenade where the sound of his practice would offend no-one. It added considerably to the already evocative atmosphere of the memorial. Erected to commemorate the death of Levassor in 1897, the monument was sculpted by Camille Lefèvre from a maquette by Aimée-Jules Dalou (1838-1902). It depicts Levassor's victory in the 1896 Paris-Marseilles race, in which he drove from Paris to Marseilles and back single handed in 48 hours 48 minutes in a twin-cylinder Panhard-Levassor car with tiller steering of the type which caused his death. (A dog ran in front of his car during a race in 1897 causing it to overturn and inflicting on Levassor internal injuries from which he died at work nine months later).

For a fairly massive piece of stone Levassor's memorial is full of life. The

Left *The invention of the bicycle was a crucial step towards the development of the motor car. This monument in Bar-Le-Duc honours Pierre and Ernest Michaux, inventors of the velocipede, predecessor of the true bicycle. A velocipede was even built with a steam engine, probably the first motorcycle.*
Right *The greatest monument to the heroic age of motor racing is the Levassor Monument at the Porte Maillot in Paris.*

driver bends low over the tiller, his mechanic beside him and cheering crowds on either side waving their hats and applauding his magnificent drive. The monument is obviously treasured by the authorities; when I first visited the gardens, one of the candlelamps on the car had been damaged, perhaps by a stone thrown by a thoughtless child. On my last visit, in mid-1979, the damage had been skilfully repaired.

A Parisian monument in a very different style recalls Léon Serpollet, pioneer of the steam car. Serpollets were perhaps the only steam cars seriously to rival petrol vehicles. They had many features of the petrol car and could generate steam rapidly, thanks to Serpollet's invention of the flash boiler: one of his racing cars was the first automobile to exceed 75 mph. Serpollet died of consumption in 1908 and his company died with him. Shortly after his death his admirers erected an elaborate and somewhat fanciful monument in the Place Saint Ferdinand, in central Paris. It depicts Serpollet, apparently dressed in a nightshirt, driving an apparently unsteerable steam car which seemed to have hit an unfortunate pedestrian in a cloth cap, and was the work of a sculptor named Jules Boucher (1870-1939).

There are monuments outside Paris too: at Wirwignes near Boulogne, stands a memorial to Giosué Guippone, killed while practising for the 1910 Coupe des Voiturettes. Guippone's car, a racing Lion-Peugeot, was a freak engendered by

Left *Boucher's monument to Léon Serpollet, in the Place St Ferdinand, Paris, is a somewhat amorphous sculpture which forms a favoured resting place for Parisian pigeons.*

Below right *Only a few roads have been named after racing drivers. This is the rue Marcel Renault in Paris; near the site of Brooklands is John Cobb Road.*

Below far right *Now chiefly remembered for the series of motor races bearing his name, James Gordon Bennett was the proprietor of the* New York Herald, *and sent Stanley to find Livingstone. This road near Paris' Bois de Boulogne is named after him.*

the voiturette racing regulations of the time, which laid down maximum dimensions for bore, but not for stroke; consequently, the racing voiturette became more and more extreme, ending up with engines so tall that the driver could not see past them but had to peer round them. Instability was a built-in problem, and Guiponne was reported to have overturned on a corner. His monument depicts in bas-relief, a cheerful, grinning individual, and also includes a representation of his car and a distraught woman draped across the base of the monument.

At the end of August 1926, during the Boulogne meeting, a memorial designed by Pierre de Soëte was unveiled in memory of Henry Matthys and his mechanic Paul Vauthier who were described on the monument as *'Victimes de progrès, morts en course*; on August 30 1925. And around the same time an elaborate monument to Léon Bollée, inventor of the *voiturette* (and of an early calculating machine), was erected in his home town of Le Mans. But even the simplest of monuments can be poignant: early in 1978, when France was covered in deep snow such as it had not seen for many years, ·I followed the route of the Paris-Madrid race of 1903, which was ended at Bordeaux because there had been so many crashes. It is difficult nowadays to imagine the atmosphere of that race as the road has changed out of all recognition in the intervening three-quarters of a century. There are still a few stretches lined by trees in the traditional French manner, but no longer does one have to navigate by the treetops above a pall of white dust thrown up by the cars in front. The little town of Bonneval, where there were some spectacular accidents in the race, is now bypassed, and the level crossing where Leslie Porter's Wolseley Beetle struck the closed gates and burst into flames, incinerating its mechanic, Nixon, has been replaced by a flyover.

But there is one point where you can still sense something of the brooding atmosphere of tragedy that lay over the race. Near the little town of Couhé-Verac stands a simple obelisk to Marcel Renault. It is no longer beside the road; the corner on which Marcel Renault left the highway while attempting to overtake another vehicle and crashed into the ditch has been straightened out, and a new banked curve passes by at some distance. The monument stands now in a layby, though the trees that marked the line of the old road are still there, you can see just how narrow was the roadway on which primitive racing cars, virtually devoid of brakes, thundered down the public highway at speeds approaching 100 mph. There used to be another memorial to Marcel Renault, erected in the Renault factory at Billancourt, near Paris, by his sorrowing brother Louis. This actually carried a life size bust of the dead motorist and a bas-relief of his car, but was destroyed during an air raid in May 1942.

Racing motorists are commemorated in England, too: Brompton cemetery, a splendidly atmospheric graveyard for the well-to-do a few minutes from Earls Court where the London Motor Show was held for so many years, contains the grave of Percy Lambert, marked by the sculpture of a broken wheel. 'Pearly', as he was known to his friends was the first man to exceed 100 miles in an hour, in 1913 at Brooklands (a brass plaque commemorating this achievement is preserved in the National Motor Museum at Beaulieu). Attempting to better his record, Lambert crashed, was killed, and buried in a coffin streamlined to match his single-seat 25 hp Talbot car. His was a similar fate to that of John Godfrey Parry Thomas, buried in Weybridge churchyard in Surrey, and killed in 1927 on Pendine Sands attempting to set up a new land speed record in his monstrous 27-litre aero-engined Babs.

When Parry Thomas was killed, it was decided that a suitable memorial would be a perpetuation of Thomas' work for suffering children at the Great Ormond Street Children's Hospital. It was decided to endow a cot, and a £1,000 subscription was raised from the readership of *The Autocar*. This enabled the permanent endowment of a cot, the money being handed over to the official trustees for charitable funds who invested the money to pay the hospital the

interest annually. Over the cot was placed the inscription 'The Babs cot. Endowed in perpetuity by readers of *The Autocar* in memory of J.G. Parry Thomas, who met his death on Pendine Sands in an endeavour to set up a world's motoring record for speed, 1927'.

The financial secretary of the hospital wrote: 'This memorial is the one which above all would have commended itself to Parry Thomas' heart, for he had a wonderful love for little children. I know that some thought a memorial in stone would have been appropriate, and this would have been so if he had been only a great sportsman, but he was far greater than that. If the dead know what is passing on the earth they have left—and who can say they do not?—Parry Thomas will be happy in the knowledge that his name is for ever linked with the great ministry of healing in this hospital.' Incidentally, prominent among the lists of subscribers to the Parry Thomas memorial fund was a Miss Barbara Cooper, who gave £20, one of the biggest donations by a private individual; can she have been the mysterious 'Babs' after whom Thomas' car was named?

On Grove Hill, in Harrow, Middlesex, is a memorial plaque commemorating what is claimed to be Britain's first fatal car crash involving the occupants of a car. This took place on February 25 1899, in a rear wheel eight-seater Daimler wagonette driven by E.R. Sewell of the Daimler Motor Company, who was killed on the spot. His passenger, Major James Richer, of the Army and Navy Stores, who were prospective purchasers of the car, died four days later without regaining consciousness. But the first car driver killed in Britain was actually Henry Lindfield, of Brighton, who died as a result of an accident with his Imperial Electric car at Purley Corner, Surrey, on February 12 1898.

In the medieval square at Monmouth stands a statue of the Honourable C.S. Rolls, co-founder of Rolls-Royce, by Goscomb John. He carries a model of the Wright Flyer aeroplane on which he made the first two-way crossing of the English Channel in 1910, and on which he was shortly afterwards killed when its tailplane collapsed in a flying contest at the Bournemouth Centenary Fête. Round the base of the monument is a series of bas-reliefs depicting events from Rolls' life; included among these is a representation of the Wolseley Beetle racing car he drove in the Gordon Bennett Cup Series in 1903.

Rolls' partner, Sir Henry Royce, is also commemorated; in the autumn of 1979 a plaque was unveiled on the wall of his house at West Wittering in Sussex where he spent his summers after the Great War; ill health had forced him to leave the Rolls-Royce factory at Derby in 1911. Rolls spent his winters in the south of France in a house he had built at Le Canadel in the Riviera. Of course, Rolls-Royce took over Bentley after the latter company had gone bankrupt in 1931; and the birth of the first Bentley car, *Ex 1*, is recorded in a plaque on the wall of a building in New Street Mews just off London's Baker Street, where the prototype was constructed in 1919. The sound of its 3-litre engine being bench tested was a cause of great annoyance and distress to the staff and inmates of the neighbouring hospital.

In America, the man who put the world on wheels is commemorated by not merely a monument but by an entire village, one of the world's biggest museums, and an historical trail. But then Henry Ford was a man who dealt in superlatives himself, having produced over 16.5 million examples of his immortal Model T between 1908 and 1928, and secured a greater proportion of the world's car market than any other constructor in the history of the motor car.

The State of Michigan has recognised a number of Henry Ford's achievements by erecting marker boards confirming them as registered historic sites. Outside the Edison Institute in Henry Ford's Greenfield Village a double-sided marker board records on one side Henry Ford's philosophy with regard to history. During the famous Chicago tribune libel trial of 1916, Ford said that he had never actually claimed that 'History is bunk'—he just claimed that he 'never needed it very bad'. Angered by claims that he was ignorant and had no feeling for history, he founded one of the world's great museums, Greenfield Village, which combines an unrivalled collection of Americana and historic vehicles with a number of historic buildings assembled from all over the States and indeed from Europe. The marker quotes Ford as saying, 'I am collecting the history of our people as written in things their hands made and used . . . Education is the greatest force in civilisation . . . I deeply admire the men who founded this country and I think we ought to know more about them and how

Above left *Parry Thomas in* Babs *in 1926, the year that this aero-engined giant took the Land Speed Record. Originally the* Higham Special, *built by Count Lou Zborowski as a successor to his famous* Chitty-Chitty-Bang-Bangs *(named for an obscene First World War song),* Babs *was fitted with a Thomas-designed streamline body.*

Right *Parry Thomas' grave in Weybridge churchyard* (John Wright).

they lived and the force and courage they had . . . the farther you look back the farther you can look ahead . . . when we are through we shall have reproduced American life as lived, and that, I think, is the best way of preserving at least a part of our history and tradition'. The other side of the marker records the opening of the Edison Institute which was dedicated to Thomas Alva Edison and opened by President Herbert Hoover on October 21 1929, the 50th anniversary of the invention of Edison's incandescent lamp.

In 1926 the City of Detroit affixed a small plaque to the outer entrance of the newly-finished Michigan Building, an office complex which stood on the site of 58, Bagley Avenue where Henry Ford built his first car, the Quadricycle, in 1896. It was here that he also created America's first garage for, finding that the door of his workshop was too narrow when he attempted to push the car out for its first road test in June 1896, he took a hatchet and enlarged the exit. The shed was subsequently removed from Bagley Avenue and reconstructed in the Ford Museum at Greenfield Village, although the Bagley Avenue house was torn down. In 1972 it was noted that the Michigan Theatre which stood on the exact site of 58, Bagley Avenue, was to be converted into America's largest night club after a brief spell as a Cinema showing X Certificate films.

One of the earliest markers to be installed by the Michigan Historical Commission was dedicated on May 26 1956 by William Clay Ford, the youngest grandson of Henry Ford, in front of the Highland Park factory which the marker describes as 'Home of Model T'. Recording that it was at Highland Park that Henry Ford began mass production of cars on a moving assembly line, the marker added that by 1915 Ford was building a million Model Ts annually and that in 1925 over 9,000 were assembled in a single day. The inscription concludes 'mass production soon moved from here to all phases of American industry and set the pattern of abundance for 20th century living'. Another marker, south-east of the intersection of Greenfield and Ford Road in

Dearborn, stated 'at this intersection stood the home in which Henry Ford was born on July 30 1863. The farmhouse was owned by Ford's parents William and Mary Ford, and in 1944 it was moved to Greenfield Village'.

Other markers are in front of the Dearborn Inn, Oakwood Boulevard, Dearborn, where in 1924 Henry Ford opened Ford Airport, started the world's first ever company airline and built the first American all-metal, multi-engined passenger aircraft, the immortal Tri-Motor. Dearborn Inn, opened in 1930, was the first-ever airport hotel. Another marker is in front of the Botsford Inn, an historic hotel and the oldest in Michigan, which was bought and restored by Henry Ford in 1924. Also surviving in the Dearborn area are Henry Ford's home, Fairlane, (now occupied by the University of Michigan) and named after the street in Cork, Ireland, where his paternal grandfather was born. It was at Fairlane that Ford died in 1947, from a cerebral haemorrhage, at the age of 84. He was buried in the Ford family burial ground on Joy Road and Greenfield Road in Detroit, beneath a simple marker slab alongside other members of the Ford family.

In 1969, a marker was erected in Hartford, Wisconsin, in front of the Chrysler Outboard Corporation's plant, to commemorate the Kissel Kar, built in Hartford from 1906 to 1931. The plaque described Kissel as: 'builders of low, graceful, sporty cars, which were style leaders for years. The Kissel Gold Bug and White Eagle Speedster achieved international acclaim and brought many celebrity purchasers to Hartford'.

In July 1923, a marble plaque was unveiled on the Pumpkinvine Pike, near Kokomo, Indiana, where, exactly 28 years before, Elwood Haynes had made his first run with a horseless carriage. The inscription claimed: 'This tablet marks the road and starting-place where Elwood Haynes, on July 4 1894, sitting in America's first car, made the initial run.' Unfortunately, it was not true: at least four cars had been built before the Haynes, the earliest being the 1891 Lambert

Left *Erected in 1980, this 'Michigan Historic Site Marker' marks the spot where the Ford Motor Company was incorporated in 1903, in the offices of Henry Ford's initial backer, a rich coal merchant named Alexander Malcomson.*

Right *Though the Opel company began selling cars in 1899 to the designs of Friedrich Lutzmann, the company was founded in 1862 by Adam Opel, who made sewing machines in a converted cowshed in Russelsheim, near Frankfurt. This plaque, recording the company's 50th anniversary in 1912, still stands in the huge modern Russelsheim factory of Opel, now General Motors' main European company.*

Left *The rear of a monument to Carl Benz, erected in 1933 by German motoring organisations.*

Right *This monument was erected in Stuttgart to commemorate the achievements of Gottlieb Daimler. It is in the garden of the house on Taubenheimstrasse where he built his first engines.*

from Ohio City, a three-wheeler with a four-stroke engine. And the first American car to lead to a production vehicle was the 1893 Duryea 'power wagon'.

In 1979, the house at Hollgasse 7, Schorndorf, near Stuttgart, where Gottlieb Daimler was born, was acquired by Daimler-Benz. The Untertürkheim motor manufacturers planned to restore the 300-year old half-timbered house completely and turn it into a memorial to Daimler. Gottlieb Daimler was born on March 17 1834, spent his childhood and youth in Schondorf and became apprenticed to a gunsmith. The house, in which there had been a bakery since 1695, was built shortly after the Thirty Years' War and was acquired by the Daimler family in 1786; Gottlieb Daimler's father also ran a bakery and a wine parlour there. The Daimler family could trace its tradition as bakers back to the 17th century. Number 7 Hollgasse was in the possession of the family over a period of three generations and ultimately it was Gottlieb's brother, Karl-Wilhelm, who ran the bakery there until 1876. This attractive half-timbered house which has a plaque on the front in memory of Gottlieb Daimler last changed hands in 1919, and for many years housed a small restaurant, the 'Daimler-Stube'.

2 The Cars

The first old car rallies

Even though the preservation of early motor vehicles had begun before the Great War, they were regarded purely as museum pieces, and certainly not as driveable vehicles. Though a few individuals bought and drove early motor cars, the majority were rather like today's custom car enthusiasts—more interested in modifying the vehicle and improving its performance than in preserving its originality. Old cars were worth almost nothing in Britain in the late 1920s and early 1930s—one carter in the Winchester area acquired an 8 hp car in good running order in exchange for six cartloads of manure!

The first run of old vehicles intended to demonstrate them as historical objects took place in Munich, Germany, on July 12 1925, to celebrate the 25th Anniversary of the Allgemeine Schnauferlklub. The club organised 'a public procession of all the ancient motor vehicles that could be collected from museums, private individuals and other sources'. Among the vehicles present were a number of early Benz cars, Daimler's 1885 motor cycle, an 1894 Hildebrand & Wolfmüller motor bicycle, and the first cars built by such pioneers as Opel and Stoewer. Early Horch and Adler cars also took part, driven by their constructors Horch and Kleyer. The first Opel of 1900 was driven by the famous racing driver Karl Joerns.

Eye witness reports claimed that 'the difficult problem to solve was to get these old cars to run or be driven under their own original power. That this was overcome was evidenced by the fact that the procession was held and included many old-stagers—musty, rusty and spider-webbed relics of the past. It is said that there were scores of fitters, mechanics and motor engineers present to induce them to start'. Carl Benz, then aged 82, was guest of honour, and demonstrated his original prototype Benz of 1885-6, which had been taken out of the Deutsches Museum at Munich for the occasion. With his son Eugen, Benz also rode on an early Benz four-wheeled Viktoria, dating from 1895. 'Great amusement was caused when the old Benz cars were started by a horizontal fly-wheel from the engine fixed in the rear portion of the carriage. When stationary, the vibration set up throughout the vehicle appeared extremely comical to present day motorists. However, when the car began to run, the trembling motion ceased as if by magic.'

Two years later, in Britain, the newspapers *Daily Sketch* and *Sunday Graphic* organised a run from London to Brighton at the instigation of their motoring correspondent, Robert W. Beare. The event was restricted to cars over 21 years of age 'in order to give modern motorists an idea of the cars on which the pioneers did their motoring.' The run started at 9 am on Sunday, November 13 1927, from the Victoria Embankment near Scotland Yard, and followed as closely as possible the route used on November 14 1896 on the original Emancipation Day Run. Before the event the cars were assembled at the premises of Auto-Auctions Ltd, in Horseferry Road, Westminster, to be examined by the judges and inspected by the public.

The judges for the event were all famous pioneer motorists: Lieutenant Colonel Charles Jarrott (former racing motorist and co-founder of the Automobile Association), S.F. Edge (another ex-racing driver and the man who put Napier cars on the map), J.S. Critchley (connected with Daimler in the early days), J.W. Stocks (a former racing cyclist who had distinguished himself at the wheel of De Dion Bouton cars), E.M.C. Instone (another distinguished former employee of Daimler) and Walter C. Bersey (who had built his first electric motor vehicle while still a teenager, and operated London's first motor cab fleet in the 1890s).

An entry of 51 vehicles was received for the run, the oldest of which was claimed to date from 1893, though it had in fact been built four or five years later. Several of the competing vehicles still survive today, and make the annual pilgrimage to Brighton, for though the 1927 run held the old cars up to a certain amount of ridicule, it was so successful that it became an annual event. The newspapers which had organised the original run referred to the competing vehicles as 'old crocks', and it took many years for the event to lose its popular title of 'The Old Crocks' Race'.

Forty-four of the vehicles entered in 1927 actually started, and 37 arrived at Brighton, with 21 making non-stop runs. The 1927 event was open to vehicles made up to 1906, but the following year (when *The Autocar* took over the organisation) the age limit was modified, so that the run was only open to cars over 25 years old. This limitation also applied in 1929, (the only year the Run took place in October) so that vehicles made up to the end of 1904 were then able to take part. The Royal Automobile Club took over the organisation in 1930, and the age limit remained fixed at 1904. It was at the end of the 1930 run that three of the entrants—S.C.H. Davis of *The Autocar*, Jackie Masters and Captain J.H. Wylie met in the Old Ship Hotel in Brighton and decided to form the world's first club for owners of old vehicles, the Veteran Car Club of Great Britain, still today the world's premier old vehicle organisation. A plaque commemorating this event was subsequently placed in the Old Ship.

So the 1927 Brighton Run, though intended as a lighthearted diversion, was the seed from which today's great interest in early motor vehicles sprang. The vehicles which took part were the first early cars to compete in a long distance road run rather than a local parade, and the full entry list is a remarkable record of the ability of the first cars to survive years of abuse. It is given below, with the dates and comments offered by the owners (though it should be noted that several of the more optimistic entrants pre-dated their vehicles by a number of years, including one hopeful who claimed to own an 1895 Renault, when the company did not come into existence for another three years!)

*   *   *

List of cars and entrants for the Run

1   Panhard & Levassor   1893   John Bryce, Lanark
2   Benz   1893-4 Donald Morrison, Gravesend
    Used to the end of the war, and not again until October 1927.
3   Benz   1894-5 Leonard D. Stears, Surbiton
    Original front tyres; back tyres put on in 1902. No new parts added in
    any way.
4   Renault   1895   Doran, Taggart & Co, Putney
5   Daimler Open Phaeton   1896   Stephen E. Statham, Baker Street,
                                        London
    Second Daimler built. The late King Edward had his trial run in this car,
    prior to ordering his first Daimler.
6   Daimler   1897   Monty Wells, Nottingham
7   Benz   1897   Mrs Mary Miles, South Croydon
    In original state as it left manufacturers, being in no way modernised.
8   Daimler   1897   George Hy. Pruen, Burnham-on-Sea
    Believed to have been in constant use all the time; anyway since 1902, to
    owner's own knowledge.
9   Panhard & Levassor   1897   G. Levrey, Fitzroy Square, London
    Bought in France in 1904; been through Germany and Belgium; running in
    England ever since. Been in use on and off for 23 years.
10 Daimler   1898   Douglas M. Copley, Birmingham
    Originally built for Daimler Manager; was on fire and then rebuilt; has
    been in use regularly. Awarded 1st prize Coventry Hospital Carnival,
    1926-7. Owner offers to race it against any car of its age with 10 people
    aboard!
11 Stephens   1898   R. Stephens & Sons, Upper Norwood
    Original in design and of British manufacture. Run continuously for
    business and pleasure until about 1908.
12 Star   1898   University Motor Ltd, Hertford St,
                                        London
13 Benz   1898   Arthur B.C. Day, Barrow-on-
                                        Humber
14 Benz   1899   William Vincent, Reading.
    In general use, and also used for cutting timber in the country.
15 Renault   1899   B.J. Smyth-Wood, Victoria
    Been to Renault works to get birth certificate! Afterwards drove across
    Town with six up.
16 Darracq   1900   William Vincent, Reading.
17 Benz   1900   Alfred Hollands, Newbury
    Bought in 1900 and driven many miles for six or seven years; has since been
    stored. With the exception of making good one or two joints and rewiring
    ignition and renewing plug, nothing has been done to it. After a rest of 17
    years, the engine started again with one or two pulls at the flywheel.
18 Benz   1900   Dr F.H. Pearse, Plymouth
    Driven from Tottenham Court Road to Plymouth on the same day as
    purchased, 27 years ago. Never failed to return home on its own power.
    All parts still as good as new.
19 Siddeley   1901   University Motors Ltd, Piccadilly,
                                        London

In constant use since 1903. Toured Scotland, Ireland and France.
Mentioned in H. Plunket Greenes' book, Where the Bright Waters Meet.

20   Panhard & Levassor   1901   G. Roger Wakeling, Brockenhurst
In hands of a Director of Panhard & Levassor in Paris 1901. In England
since about 1902-3. Coil ignition fitted 1903-4; pneumatic tyres after the
War.

21   Panhard & Levassor   1901   Alain Norman L. Maclachlan,
                                            Basingstoke
Believed to have been in pieces in a garage in Henley for 14 years. Five or
six years ago it was put together and made to go.

22   De Dion Bouton   1902   Vincent Ballardini, Brighton
Working in Brighton every day.

23   De Dion   1902   Geo. Burtenshaw, Reigate.
24   Renault   1902   T.F. Morris, Herne Bay.
Car still runs on accumulator and coil with float carburettor; no alterations
have been made to body or engine.

25   Clement Talbot   1902   Doran, Taggart & Co, Putney
26   Lanchester   1902   T. Hamilton-Adams, Pall Mall,
                                            London
27   De Dion Bouton   1902-4   Arthur Woods, Hythe, Kent
In constant use for the last 12 years—running every day.

28   Oldsmobile   1903   General Motors Ltd, The Hyde,
                                            London
29   De Dion   1903   A. Spicer & Co Ltd, East Sheen.
Still running—mostly original parts.

30   De Dion Bouton   1903   E.F. Richardson, Purley.
Ran to Crediton (Exeter) from Lewes, nearly 200 miles each way, averaging
15-16 mph; consumption 40 mpg.

31   Renault   1903   William Vincent, Reading
32   Cadillac   1903   F.S. Bennett, St John's Wood
Completed with honours and winning cups in Sunrising Hill-climb 1903;
RAC Reliability Trial 1903; Blackpool Speed Tests 1904. In 1913, under
RAC observation, exactly 10 years after, it re-ran the RAC 1,000 miles trial
in which it made history.

33   Sunbeam   1903   W.H. Cocks, Weybridge
Has been in constant use without repairs of any importance.

34   Riley   1903   Victor E. Leverett, N. Audley St,
                                            London
35   Rover   1903-5   W.E. Watson, S. Kensington
'Boanerges'—City and Guilds College mascot.

36   Wolseley   1904   G.F. Surtees, Lowestoft
Took 1st prize in the Comic Car section at the Lowestoft carnival. On
exhibition at the Wolseley showrooms in Piccadilly, making the journey
from Lowestoft to London by road.

37   Vauxhall (Single cylinder)   1904   Percy C. Kidner, W. Hampstead
38   Mercedes   1904   Joseph Polledri, Kingston-on-Thames
39   De Dion Bouton   1904   W.J. Baker, Honor Oak Park
40   Humber (Beeston)   1905   James Stringfellow, Wombwell
41   Cadillac   1905   General Motors Ltd, The Hyde,
                                            London

42   Rover (Single cylinder)   1905   Miss O. Dawes, Coventry
     Mostly original parts.
43   Fiat   1906   John Stubberfield, Eastbourne
     Twenty-one years' constant hard work. Not one mechanical breakdown
     during the last 70,000 miles. 16 hp; weighs 1 ton; will carry eight people
     200 miles a day.
44   Renault   1906   G. Eggleton, Watford
     Has been in regular use since 1906, and is still working daily as hackney
     carriage. One universal coupling replaced and Zenith carburettor fitted.
45   Rover   1906   Wm Heckman & Sons, Henley-on-
                                           Thames
     In constant use until 1913.
46   Wolseley Siddeley (2-   1906   T.H.L. Salisbury, Bristol
     cylinder)
     Has done about 45,000 miles all over England.
47   Rolls-Royce   1906   Dawson K. Bunn, Newman St,
                                           London
     Modernised with four-seater sports body. Original engine, clutch, gear
     and wheels.
48   De Dion Bouton   1906   C.H. Boffin, Middle Barton, Oxon
     Converted into small van, and used daily since September 1922.
49   Argyll (with Aster engine)   1906   G.W. Looker, Stanford-le-Hope
50   Panhard   1906   Joseph Walters, Belgravia
     Originally in private use, then turned into a van. Last 10 years in possession
     of entrant; in constant use for goods. Convertible to 10-12 seater.
51   Renault   1906   T.L. Stopps, Beaconsfield
     Delivered to the late Queen Alexandra in 1906; used by her until her death,
     and afterwards licensed by HM King George. Car was used by Her Majesty
     on Rose Days.

*   *   *

The 1928 Run saw the first overseas entrants, Jean Terouanne and Robert
Treille from France, with a Léon Bollée voiturette 'which unfortunately could
not compete as it was brought over from France after entries had closed, but it
made the journey unofficially, its driver and passenger obviously surprised at
the reception accorded them!' Nowaways, veteran car owners bring their vehicles
from all over the world to compete in 'The Brighton'.

The Brighton Run has grown in stature over the years, and now attracts an
entry—limited by the police—of some 300 vehicles annually. Successful
competitors, who manage to reach Brighton within eight hours, are presented
with a bronze medal which is a replica of that awarded to the contestants in the
1896 event, and bearing the Goddess of Speed emblem of H.J. Lawson's motor
car syndicate. They are not so fortunate, however, as the 37 successful entrants
in the 1927 Brighton who were awarded a specially struck gold medal, while the
three 'most meritorious performers' were given substantial cash prizes in
addition. Nowadays, the London to Brighton entrants undertake the journey as
a matter of course; certainly it is the world's premier motoring event, attracting
an estimated three million spectators annually, far more than any rally or Grand
Prix event for modern cars.

Categories of collectable car

Veteran (up to December 31 1904)

These are the true ancestors of the motor car. The veteran period encompasses perhaps the widest variety of motor car, because progress took place so rapidly during that period. Therefore veteran cars range from primitive motorised tricycles, like the De Dion Bouton, to sophisticated cars capable of over 90 mph such as the 60 hp Mercedes. In relation to other collectable cars, the smaller veterans have not shown such an alarming rate of appreciation in recent years. Their power output is minimal, but in general they are extremely well put together, even if the logic of their engineering is sometimes a little strange. Most popular of the small veterans is the De Dion Bouton, with a single cylinder 6 or 8 hp engine in the front under a crocodile bonnet. De Dion furnished engines to many other assemblers of cars at this period and their rate of production at their Puteaux factory was so great that if an engine failed to run on the final test bench, it was immediately torn down and its spare parts used once again on the production line, as there was not enough time to search for an elusive fault. The most powerful veterans, such as the Mercedes or the De Diétrich, can be worth a very great deal of money indeed as there are so few of them and they offer the exquisite workmanship of the early 20th century, coupled with perhaps the most exciting performance characteristics of all; however, braking is generally not their strong point.

Edwardian (1905 to December 31 1918)

Though it is somewhat inaccurate historically, the portmanteau term 'Edwardian' covers some of the most elegant motor cars ever built. Because the cut-off date for the veteran category is so arbitrary, there is a fair amount of

In the first decade of this century, the steam car was a serious rival to the petrol car, but faded away because it was more complex to drive and maintain. These 1905 Serpollet cars (classed as Edwardians) show that, despite their undisputed advantages of speed and uncanny silence, steam cars had to disguise themselves as petrol cars to be acceptable to the car-buying public.

The 'Alfonso XIII' Hispano-Suiza was one of the great Edwardian sporting cars. This 1913 example, seen at the sale of the A.W.F. Smith collection in the mid-1960s, once belonged to motoring journalist, William Boddy.

carry over between the two periods with little single cylinder cars such as the De Dion or the Oldsmobile Curved Dash Runabout being made up until 1907-8 and high performance models such as the big Mercedes being progressively developed from 1901 on. Again, the bigger cars of this period, especially those from the well-known marques like Rolls-Royce, are worth a king's ransom, for they represent a blending of engineering skill, consumate craftsmanship and elegance of line which has never been matched. They are a link with an age that came to an end with the outbreak of the Great War and epitomise motoring at its very best, in an era when the common currency was still gold and little traffic cumbered the roads. The Edwardian era also saw the introduction of the immortal Model T Ford, the car which put the world on wheels and introduced the concept of mass-production on a moving assembly line, and the birth of refined small cars with well-engineered four-cylinder engines and roomy tourer bodies. Designers such as the Yorkshireman, Owen Clegg, who worked both for Rover and for Darracq, created family cars which became legendary for their neat finish and longevity. Another class of vehicle which appeared at this time was the cycle car, heralded as the provider of 'Motoring for the Million' and by utilising motorcycle engines in skimpily built chassis, either of wood or steel tubing, gave rapid transport with a fair amount of personal risk and an almost total disregard of normal engineering criteria.

Vintage (1919 to 1930)

The vintage period saw the motor car achieve maturity. During this period not only were some of the finest and most brilliantly engineered motor cars constructed, but motoring became a commonplace occurrence, rather than the pastime of a privileged few. Popular cars such as the Austin Seven and Bullnose Morris in England, the Cloverleaf Citroën and the Fiat 509 in Europe, joined

Some vintage cars incorporated design features regarded as advanced even today: these front-wheel-drive Alvises, with independent front suspension, competed in the 1928 Le Mans 24-hour race.

the Model T Ford in bringing motoring to the masses. Luxury vehicles such as the H6B Hispano 32 cv overhead camshaft six-cylinder and the straight-eight Isotta Fraschini became legends in their own time. The 1930s were, too, the last period when independent small constructors could successfully maintain a foothold in the popular car market in the face of the mass-producers. The Depression and the rise in registrations of cars built in great numbers on moving production lines served to put even the most consistent of these independents out of business by the early 1930s. Ford's revolutionary invention of a moving production line took perhaps a decade to find its way into other factories, but once it was installed, it proved to be a most powerful weapon in the sales war, enabling manufacturers to meet an ever growing demand while holding down their prices. Nevertheless, there were some surprising examples of obstinacy in the face of progress. While William Morris had a moving production line in his body shop in the mid-1920s, and pioneered the use of all-metal construction, he was content to adhere to the old method of chassis building whereby the chassis were pushed from work station to work station by hand and assembled where they stood on the floor. He did not adopt a moving line in the chassis shop until 1932. The harsh economic climate of the latter part of the 1920s left its mark on the design and construction of motor cars, and in general, cars made after 1927 do not have quite the same appeal as earlier models. Some of the blame for this can be laid at the door of the car stylist, Harley Earl, who in 1927 introduced the concept of the annual model change by creating the LaSalle V8 for General Motors in the image of Hispano Suiza. Only the biggest companies could keep up with the enormous costs involved in completely redesigning their model line every year and, in the search for novelty of appearance, the old standards of styling were sometimes let slip.

Post Vintage Thoroughbred (1931 to 1940)

A very tendentious definition this, with eligibility in theory limited to certain makes specified by the Vintage Sports Car Club Committee. These are the cars which are felt not to have compromised their standards of design, construction and performance during the depressed 1930s, when styling began to take over from engineering as a prime selling force and the materials used in the construction of a motor car were generally not of the same quality as those used in vintage models. However, in recent years, the rise in price of vintage cars—most vintage models now sell for between £4,000 and £40,000—has prompted a growing interest in the cheaper cars of the period. Some of these, like the 'smallbore' Fords and the Morris Eight, were well-built little vehicles, and enjoy something of a cult following. But some low-priced models of the 1930s were pretty dreary. Construction standards deteriorated during the decade, and the wood used for the body framing was not properly seasoned, and therefore rotted much more easily than on vintage models. At their best, cars of the 1930s are magnificent: at their worst they can be dull and meretricious.

Classic

To an American, a Classic is one of a select breed of quality cars built between 1925 and 1942: to a Briton, the word means something quite different. Nowadays, 'classic' can be applied indiscriminately to almost any car which is out of production—one commentator describes it as 'any car without syncro-mesh on bottom gear'. The fastest growing facet of the old car hobby, it is also the most fraught with pitfalls for the unwary. Modern unit-construction cars can be unbelievably expensive to restore, and are far more difficult to work on than the older vehicles. They do not, in the main, call for any special driving skills, and may have rather dreadful handling characteristics. They also, being built from Atomic Age recycled steel, bear the seeds of corruption in their structure, and will not survive like pre-war cars. But the portmanteau term 'classic' also includes magnificent machinery like the XK Jaguars, Ferraris, Ford GTs and Pegaso.

Discovering old cars

As ye seek, so shall ye find: to hear old vehicle enthusiasts talk, you would think that nowadays the supply of early cars had virtually dwindled to nothing, and that no significant new discoveries remained to be made. This is, however, palpably untrue. It is still possible to discover early cars which have been locked away and forgotten, and many unique vehicles continue to come to light. As I write this I know of a Lagonda, a Model A Ford and a Trojan, all within five minutes' drive of my home. All are preserved by their owners for one reason or another, yet have not been on the road for many years. Owners often put vehicles away with little thought for their preservation, just retaining them for sentimental reasons. Under such circumstances, cars are bound to deteriorate especially if they are kept in damp conditions.

I remember once visiting a small rural garage which had been closed down before the Second World War, and being shown the remains of two or three cars, including an early Rover, which the proprietor had kept at the bottom of the yard. Over the years the cars had sunk into the ground and the brambles had grown up over them; what remained was not even fit to be used as patterns for spare parts. On the other hand in 1980 a Veteran Car Club member unearthed a totally original 1919 Sunbeam that had been stored in a barn for 40 years.

In the late 1960s old cars were still being found in unlikely places with

Above *France is still fertile old-car country: this sound, if dilapidated, 5 cv Citroën was unearthed in the Beaujolais mountains in 1979.*

Opposite *In the mid-1960s the author discovered this 1920 Augus-Sanderson in a woodyard in Tenterden, Kent, where it was being used as a timber tractor. Some years later the car was rescued by a Veteran Car Club member for restoration.*

Below *Found in a rubbish dump behind a Surrey railway station, this 1928 Singer with 'As-U-Dryve' convertible coachwork was photographed by the author in the late 1960s.*

surprising ease. I recall, for example, around 1964 finding a complete vintage Morgan three-wheeler chassis abandoned on a rural rubbish tip—we brought it home in the tonneau of my 1927 Clyno, with a couple of helpers sitting on the front of the chassis to stop it tipping out over the tail! Stopping for petrol in the village of Gomshall, Surrey, in 1964 in my Clyno, I was informed by the garage owner that in the vicinity was an Edwardian Rolls-Royce Silver Ghost, which had been in the same family for three generations and which, though it had been taken off the road many years before, was kept on blocks and ceremonially started and run once a year.

I came across a similar instance about the same time at Cockfosters, North London, when I went to interview a gentleman who had a famous ex-Brooklands racing Morgan three-wheeler. He had kept the 4½-litre Bentley he had bought before the war, in pristine condition, in a local lock-up garage where it stood on blocks covered with blankets. It had last run the day war was declared when its owner drove it at 100 mph across Stag Lane Aerodrome, where he had been a pilot test flying De Havilland Moths. Since then the car had been in storage, though it was taken out once a year and towed round the block in order that oil could be forced to all its moving parts to prevent corrosion. The car was remarkably original, even down to the black locking rings on the wire wheels.

In 1966 a 1916 Model T Ford was found on a Hampshire rubbish tip and an Edwardian Sizaire Naudin was discovered in a nettle bed behind a barn, in the same county. In 1941 a Mercedes 60 hp was discovered in a building in Queens, Manhattan. It had been stored for almost 40 years. Owners were 'famed naval architects' William Francis Gibbs and his brother Frederic H. Gibbs. In 1964, the Mercedes, with a low-slung four-seat sporting body of later date than the chassis, was restored. In 1968 it was recorded as 'resting high up in an office building in Manhattan, enshrined in a secret panelled-in room, under safe lock and key from the eyes of the uninitiated and gross multitude'. A Rolls-Royce Silver Ghost in the collection of Count Raben-Levetzau in Denmark was found 'walled up' behind books in his home, Aalholm Castle. In 1968 a number of early cars was discovered in a Maples furniture depository in London; these included a 1903 De Diétrich and a 1908 Mercedes, both of which were subsequently restored to full running order.

In the summer of 1966 I was travelling home by train to Sussex reading an old car book when the gentleman sitting next to me asked me if I was interested in old cars and, after telling me that he was a former employee of Sheffield-Simplex, told me of a 1904 Sunbeam four-cylinder engine that was still providing electric power for a Sussex garage. This was apparently somewhere in the Forest Row area, though he was reluctant to be pressed further on the location of the power unit. Coupled to a dynamo used only in emergencies, the engine had been removed from the chassis many years before and its owner did not bother to overhaul it in any way so that as time passed the cylinders began to cut out so that by 1966 it was only running on one cylinder. It was in the Forest Row area, too, that the chassis members of a vintage Bean tourer were used to make the base of a wooden bridge across a river on a private estate. This I was told by Woolf Barnato's former chauffeur who lived at that time in Forest Row and still had a hub cap which he had retrieved from the wreck of the eight-litre Bentley that went over the top of the Byfleet banking at Brooklands in 1932, killing its driver Clive Dunfee.

In 1923 this Montier-Ford 'Type Gaillon' ran in the first Le Mans 24-hour race, and actually managed to finish. Some 57 years later the author photographed what was claimed to be the same car in a shed in Normandy.

Above *An impressive straight-eight Austro-Daimler saloon of the late 1920s, photographed in a French barn in early 1980.*

Below *This beautifully restored 10 hp 1902 Gladiator was discovered in derelict condition as a display on top of a garage, from where it had to be rescued by crane.*

In the 1960s I visited Sir George White, grandson of the famous 'tramway king' of Bristol. In the motor house of his home near Bristol stood a white Panhard of circa 1903 vintage. In the family since new, it had been operated until the early 1930s, when it had been put up on blocks. Sir George also told me that he did not propose to use it but to hand it over to his son so that it could truly be said to be a one owner car.

Some intriguing vehicles have been used as tractors in sports grounds, despite the commercial availability of such vehicles as the Patterson and Allen-Taylor conversions of Ford chassis produced in the 1920s and 30s. A Bournemouth skating rink used a vintage Bullnose Morris to maintain the surface of the ice, while in the 1930s an early Ford V8 was cut down for a similar purpose. Around 1962 another Bullnose Morris was in use as a sports ground tractor at Warlingham, Surrey, but the prize in this field is surely the Edwardian Regal Underslung, discovered in the 1970s by a Veteran Car Club member, which had been converted to drive a cricket pitch roller. Fortunately the modifications carried out to the vehicle were not so drastic as to prevent its restoration.

Dead and buried

It is a curious thing, but early motor cars have often been buried after their useful lifespan is over. Surprising, because it takes a considerable amount of effort to dig a hole large enough to take a motor car. Yet in several well attested cases, this is just what has happened. It all started, I suppose, with the immense gyrocar which Count Peter Schilovsky built for the Wolseley Motor Car Company before the Great War. This two wheeled giant, poised delicately by the aid of spinning gyroscopes, worked far better than it appeared to have any right to. But it must have been awkward to store, and consequently the Wolseley directors decided to get rid of it. However, as the Count presumably had some claim to the design, they decided to get rid of it in such a way that it could always be recovered if necessary. So they dug a hole in the factory yard and buried the gyrocar. Over the years, a railway siding was laid over the grave of the gyrocar and it seemed that it would never be resurrected. However, in the 1930s it was unearthed again, and restored to take its place in the company museum. But sometime after the Second World War, when the Wolseley directorate really should have known better, orders were given that it should be scrapped and this time, it seems that the job was carried out (although in the 1960s there were certainly rumours that the gyrocar had not been destroyed but hidden away and was in the secret store of a car collector).

The gyrocar was just the beginning. When Parry Thomas, the famous Welsh racing driver, crashed and was killed on Pendine Sands in 1927, his wrecked 27-litre motor car *Babs* was buried in a grave on the edge of the beach. As a military establishment was subsequently set up on that site, it seemed that *Babs* would never be seen again. But in the mid 1960s, a Welsh school teacher, Owen Wyn Owen, obtained permission to search for the remains of *Babs*. He unearthed the car, surprisingly in restorable condition after its many years in the beach, and has subsequently returned the chassis to running condition, though the streamlined aluminium bodywork of the car had corroded beyond recall and only a few patches of the car's skin were left. These were perhaps the 'glamour' interments, the ones that made headlines at the time in the motoring press. But there were many other, more humble burials, such as the Clyno saloon that was buried in the Bedfordshire village of Houghton Regis some years back. And, in the early 1930s, when compulsory insurance for motor vehicles was introduced and new rates assessments brought in for sheds used to house motor cars, a number of owners of early cars, which they had kept running on a shoestring, decided that the cost of insuring or housing these veterans was excessive, and buried them.

In March 1931, for example, Dr Francis Pearse of Plymouth, faced under a new assessment with paying £2 10s rates on the shed in which he kept his 4½ hp Benz, bought in 1900, threatened to bury the car, the first to be owned in Plymouth. He could not sell the car locally and the Plymouth museum did not want it. But veteran car enthusiast, C.S. Burney, rescued the Benz 'from an untimely grave' and ran it in Veteran Car Club events, even racing it at Brooklands. And then there was pioneer motorist Douglas Copley of Sheldon, Birmingham, with an 1898 Daimler car, who deposited the car in a deep pit with the aid of a block and tackle rather than pay rates on premises to accommodate it permanently. Oddly enough, the car (once the property of Daimler's foreman, Wormald) appears to have been reincarnated as it had been heavily modified in 1902, with features such as a modern radiator; it still competes in the annual London to Brighton run. And a Vipen, a Panhard copy built in Hull, was said to be buried on Hindhead.

There were more macabre reasons for burying the motor cycle of Arthur Moorhouse, who crashed while attempting records at Brooklands in 1912. Moorhouse went out of control and his head struck one of the telegraph poles

In 1931 Douglas Copley of Sheldon, Birmingham, was reported to have buried his 1898 Daimler rather than pay rates on its shed. However, the car seems to have been 'disinterred' subsequently to compete in veteran car events.

alongside the Railway Straight; his friends rushed up, but could do nothing to help. One of them recalled 60 years later 'There was poor Arthur's helmet with half his head inside it! It was dreadful!' The remains of Moorhouse's Indian V-twin were buried beside the Railway Straight, and may well still be there to this day.

An even more unpleasant Brooklands interment was accorded the racing Sunbeam of Dario Resta which skidded off the track and crashed through the corrugated iron fencing bordering the notorious Brooklands sewage farm. It seems that no-one attempted to recover the vehicle, which, depending on the preservative power of vintage sewage, could still be buried there. According to one Brooklands habitué, Resta's head also found its final resting place in the sewage farm. But if that is so, why is it that Resta's shattered goggles are today on exhibition in the National Motor Museum at Beaulieu? The story seems as apochryphal as that told the author by the son of the proprietor of one of the Brooklands pubs, who claimed that when playing with a friend at Brooklands in 1913, he observed Percy Lambert's fatal crash. The two boys were among the first to reach the wreckage, and my informant told me, with a spine-chilling tone in his voice, how they had discovered Lambert's goggles lying on the Brooklands banking with the driver's eyes still inside them!

Several years ago, I met an octogenarian named J.A. Turner, who was descended from Rowley Turner, who had brought the first bicycle to Britain in 1868. Mr Turner, who had chronicled his life in the motor industry in painstaking detail in a great pile of hand-written books, had, in the late 1920s taken many ancient cars in part exchange which had little or no resale value, save as scrap. The problem was disposal of the vehicles. It was solved in a novel way by driving the cars to a water filled gravel pit in the Staines area, stripping them of everything saleable, starting the engine, chocking out the clutch with a piece of wood, setting the engines to run fast, and then, from a safe distance, pulling away the chock with a piece of string, letting the car roar over the brink of the gravel pit at full throttle and vanish beneath the water. Mr Turner disposed of many cars in this way, and it is possible that reclamation of the gravel pits could uncover their remains. However, they are likely to be in a poor condition due to the intake of water into the engine.

There are other well attested instances of watery graves for motor cars: in the early 1960s, the American magazine *Antique Automobile* recorded discovery of a vintage Rolls-Royce in a deep lake. The car had apparently been driven, or pushed, into the lake after a gangland killing in the 1920s, and it was said that when it was recovered, a nickel plated revolver was found beneath the front seat. A little later, divers working in Stockholm harbour in Sweden discovered the remains of an Edwardian Gräf und Stift 40 hp touring car which seemed to have withstood its submersal beneath the Baltic remarkably well; in fact, one of the steel studded Dunlop tyres still held air and there was petrol still in the carburettor! The same conditions which had preserved the wooden war ship, the *Vasa*, seemed to have protected the car, which was subsequently restored. Stockholm harbour, it seems, was a favourite dumping ground for people who wanted to get rid of obsolete motor vehicles.

Another burial at sea is more intriguing, perhaps. When, in 1932, Ford introduced the famous 8 hp Model Y, 14 hand-built prototypes were exhibited at selected locations across Europe. The development programme had been perhaps the most rapid in the history of motoring, in fact the first design sketches had only been made in October 1931. The shows were what, in modern parlance, are known as 'clinics' at which the reactions of public and dealers to new designs were noted, and the vehicle altered accordingly before it entered production the following August. Having served their purpose the prototype Model Ys were of no further use. The one which was shown in Oslo appeared to have been taken into Norway in such haste that the proper customs formalities had not been completed. And in those days tarriff barriers meant that the car could not be taken out of the country again without payment of heavy duty. But the car was not to remain in the country either, for that too would incur a tax penalty. The dilemma was neatly solved by burying the car at sea, a safe distance out from the shore . . . where it presumably remains.

When in 1924 the Red River threatened to burst its banks and inundate the town of Shreveport, Louisiana, 2,000 old cars were bought and sunk in the river to act as a temporary flood barrier until a permanent one could be constructed. And when the stretch of macadam roadway 100 feet long by 50 feet wide collapsed at Thompsonville, Connecticut, early in 1928, the local authorities found the hole too big to fill by normal means. They therefore bought 250 'junk' cars at prices from $5 to $10 to fill the hole. One wonders what priceless relics now form part of the local roadbed. In September 1930, a member of Bridlington Town Council's General Purposes Committee complained that 50-60 old car chassis had been used to strengthen the foundations of the new north sea wall then under construction. And in the 1970s, a deep-sea diver found a sunken ship with a cargo of Great War Model T Fords and Douglas motorcycles off Newhaven in Sussex. The brass parts had survived, but the ferrous components were corroded beyond recall.

A slightly macabre piece of underwater automobile archaeology was revealed in 1966, when a Mr Joseph Quilty presented the windscreen frame of his father's 20 hp Briscoe tourer to President De Valera of Ireland. The car was being used by a party of volunteers from Dublin and Limerick on the night of Good Friday 1916 when they set out to dismantle the Cahirciveen wireless station and re-erect it at Tralee to help guide in a ship carrying German arms and Irish patriots at the direction of Roger Casement. However, the volunteers missed the way and the car plunged over the edge of the Ballykissane pier on the River Lanne, near Killorglin. Three of the occupants were drowned, though the driver survived, and the windscreen was recovered from the wreck.

In 1965 a scrap yard in the British Midlands installed an hydraulic car crusher for dealing with scrap vehicles. One of the first vehicles put into this crusher was a 1932 Austin in original condition whose elderly lady owner had owned the vehicle since new and was determined that no one should drive the car but herself. To that end she had the car compressed into a metallic cube which she announced would be used as her headstone when she was buried. But perhaps the strangest automotive burial of all was that specified by the American lady Ferrari enthusiast who left instructions in her will that she was to be buried seated in her car in her nightdress!

Breaking up old cars

Today's car breakers' yards tend to be full of the rusting shells of modern mass-produced cars piled in great heaps, of no interest to anyone except the marginal motorist looking for spare parts. However, those whose memories go back only

This circa 1929 Delage coupé was photographed in Brooks' breakers yard at Edenbridge, Kent, in 1958. Round the corner were four Edwardian Rolls-Royce Silver Ghosts piled in a heap.

as far as the 1950s will remember that in those days car breakers' premises were mostly occupied by cars of the 1930s with the occasional earlier gem standing forlornly in their midst. A modern factory now occupies the site of the old Brooks yard at Edenbridge in Kent; a visit to this yard in the late 1950s revealed no fewer than four Rolls-Royce Silver Ghosts standing one upon the other, and, complete and apparently driveable, a big Daimler saloon and a very elegant vintage Delage. Goodey's yard at Twyford in Berkshire (shut down in the late 1960s) was another mecca for seekers after parts for rare and obscure cars. Part of the outer fence of Harold Goodey's premises was formed from the wing panels of a 1920s military biplane, possibly a Westland Wapiti. Inside, there were great piles of spares for all sorts of motor cars, while in sheds round the yard could be found complete vehicles, many of them of great rarity. In fact, Mr Goodey was instrumental in preserving many early vehicles, including the curious Thames stagecoach now on show in the National Motor Museum in Beaulieu, and supplied cars to John Sword's collection in Scotland. Around 1962, Goodey's sheds housed such *rara aves* as a Voisin two-seater and a number of veterans. There were many other such establishments, including that of the old gentleman of Wrotham Hill in Kent whose premises yielded a number of early vehicles and whose inner sanctum in an unprepossessing shed was filled with an Aladdin's Cave of early lamps, horns and magnetos.

The demise of such establishments coincided with the rise of price in early motor cars, when the destruction of old motor cars for scrap metal value became less profitable than selling the remains to an enthusiast for restoration. In 1927, the same year that saw the birth of the old car preservation movement with the holding of the first London to Brighton Run for veteran cars, a car breaker set down his methods of operation and commented that: 'Being broken up for scrap must account for at least 75 per cent of old cars. The remainder fade away as cheap runners to outlying districts where space is not important, and when they break down, there they stay. We recently removed a car that for years had stopped a gap in a hedge.'

On the business side of car breaking, the same man noted: 'The majority of cars cost the breaker between £2 and £7 in scrap value alone; the sale price of parts is not governed by their cost but by the cost of selling them. Consideration will show that if one were presented gratis with a couple of acres of spare parts it would still be possible to trade at a loss, even if 10 per cent could be sold a year. So we arrived at fairly set prices, of which I append a few average figures: complete rear axle £3 15s; ditto gearbox £2 15s; piston 8s 6d; crankshaft £2; roadspring 8s 6d; ball races 1s 6d to 8s 6d.

'We collect cars in a radius of about 30 miles, one scrap car towing another, often minus tyres and frequently brakeless. On arrival the car is categorised: as of good saleability of parts, when the metal only is removed, the rest of the chassis being dumped in the open; fair saleability, when the metal, frame, front axle etc are scrapped, working parts stored under cover, and rear axle in the open; and no saleability when the entire car is scrapped. Complete scrapping saves almost exactly 50 per cent on time.

'In complete scrapping, wings are removed with a sledgehammer, while the body is removed, often by breaking the wood from the bolts. The radiator is removed in the usual way, reduced to brass and run into ingots. The body is reduced to its hair (if any), leather, iron, glass, etc, in about one hour's time. Cylinders are removed in the usual way, and a tap on each piston head leaves the crankcase and gearbox for attention. After the usual disconnection, further

Left *L. Hunt's 'Vale of the White Horse Cycle & Engineering Works' was one of the earliest motor repair establishments in England, having attended its first breakdown in 1897. In 1910 the firm was using this highly-modified Benz Viktoria of c 1898 vintage as a utility vehicle. Mr Hunt's son, who had started work in the 1880s as red flag boy to the North Oxfordshire Steam Ploughing Company, provided the author with many reminiscences of 19th century motoring.*

Right *Early cars had little value in the 1920s, when this ancient racing car was being used as a rather unlikely furniture van.*

sledge blows on the bearer arms remove these. The hammer and sett part the axles, frame, and springs, and the frames are periodically cut up with oxygen.

'The final process is the segregation of metal, which must be cleaned before dispatch. A fire is made of the tyres, body wood, grease and oil, and the crankcase and gearbox placed on top. At the critical heat at which the metal becomes brittle it is removed with hammer and tongs. The metal is bagged up and the registered number of the car sent in for cancellation.'

These depressing statistics reveal why so few early cars survive. Depreciation made them more valuable reduced to their basic elements than as complete vehicles. Many very early cars were still in regular use at that time by owners who took no heed of fashion, but such cars were difficult to sell, as there were few active searchers for veteran vehicles at that period, and early cars were destroyed by the dozen. Indeed, in America Henry Ford bought thousands of old cars of every make at a flat rate of $20 to be reduced to scrap and melted down to manufacture more Model Ts. It was only in the latter part of the 1920s that he began to preserve early vehicles as part of his huge museum of Americana he was then setting up at Greenfield Village.

However, though the breakers did destroy many rare and irreplaceable vehicles, at least one of their number became one of the world's leading collectors of historic vehicles. Henri Malartre, of Lyons, was working in the family scrap metal business in the late 1920s when an early Rochet Schneider was brought to him to be broken up. M. Malartre was so impressed with the condition of the old car that he decided to preserve it, and it formed the nucleus of his collection which is today housed in the Château de Rochetaillé, north of Lyons.

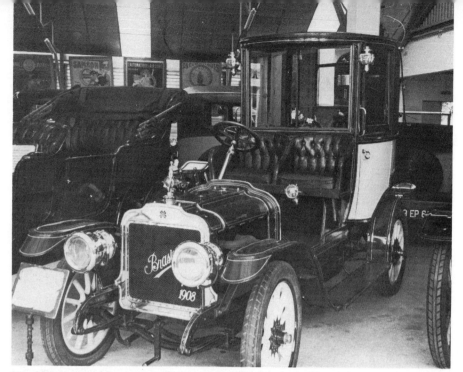

The Rochetaillée museum preserves many vehicles built in the Lyons region, such as this 1908 Brasier 10/12 hp coupé de ville.

Dating a car

Perhaps no subject can cause more ill feeling and heated tempers in old car circles than the dating and authentication of early vehicles. The reason for this is simple; because certain arbitrary age limits have been established, the year of construction of a vehicle can determine whether or not it is eligible for prestige events like the annual London to Brighton Veteran Car Run and consequently its value can be enhanced or depreciated. In fact, one can question the advisability of establishing purely arbitrary and inflexible date divisions for early cars, for there was inevitably an overlap of production. It seems illogical to classify a car built on December 31 1904 as a veteran and thus eligible for the Brighton Run, while an identical vehicle built a few hours later on January 1 1905 is by definition an Edwardian and ineligible. The broad classifications—Veteran, Edwardian and Vintage—serve only to define certain concepts and their rigid applications has led to cases of faking early cars so that they will qualify for one category or another. Such cases are fortunately rare, but there have been cases of cars being altered to incorporate mechanical features that have secured them a certificated date, in some cases earlier than the start of production of that model by the factory that built them! There have also been instances of cars having their original construction plates prised off, their engine numbers filed away and new numbers and new plates made to give them the semblance of having been built some years earlier.

Serious attempts to date early motor cars accurately were first made in 1932, when the two year old Veteran Car Club received lists of information from De Dion, Benz and Panhard, which enabled them to fix the date of manufacture of many early cars. The Veteran Car Club, having gathered the evidence, and members of the circle of 19th century motorists, who had driven such cars at the turn of the century, checked the vehicles to verify that they were what they claimed to be and then dating certificates were issued to verify the car's eligibility for entry in the Brighton Run.

The reason why 1904 was chosen as the definite cut-off date for veteran motor cars seems to have been that when *The Autocar* took over the organisation of the Run in 1928 and 1929, the event was restricted to cars over 25 years old. However, in 1930, the organisation passed to the Royal Automobile Club, who have run it ever since, and they merely froze the existing regulations as they had existed in 1929. It seems as though the 1904 date was purely a matter of administrative convenience for the Royal Automobile Club, and it is interesting to speculate what might have happened had *The Autocar* continued to organise the Run. If the 25 year limit had continued to be applied up to the present day, by now vehicles such as Ford Mark I Consuls and Standard Vanguards would be classified as veterans. Indeed, among a very large section of the public the popular misconception that eligibility for the Brighton Run is governed by a sliding date still persists; for the past 20 years I have often been asked when my 1927 Clyno will become 'eligible for the Brighton Run'.

The 1904 date was established when the science of dating early vehicles was much less refined and I cannot think of any logical reason for its retention. That date has now become as immutable as the laws of the Medes and Persians, and about as relevant. Indeed, if one has to choose a year to end the veteran classification, 1905 would seem to have more going for it, as it was more of a watershed in the early history of the car. That was the year when the French, having won the Gordon Bennett Race for the second year in succession, brought the series to an end. As that was the prestige event of the motoring year, its termination brought something of an emotional shock. Its replacement in 1906

A curious example of the lengths that manufacturers of replicas and 'look-alikes' will go to is this '1898 Panhard' photographed in 1971. Built by a French company rejoicing in the name of 'Le Bastard', who also built replicas of pre-Great War Paris buses, this 'veteran' is actually based on a Land-Rover chassis!

by the Grand Prix (which the French manufacturers suspended in 1908 because the German Mercedes car had won it and upset the myth of French superiority) brought an entirely different atmosphere to international competition, which even then had become the shop window for national industries. Equally, many designs overlapped quite amazingly, and perhaps it would be fairest on all counts to include as veterans, cars which were introduced during the veteran period and manufactured without alteration beyond its confines.

The definition of a veteran car as having been manufactured prior to the end of 1904 is not universally agreed. When the British government amended its construction and use regulation in 1963, new legislation quickly followed to ensure that certain veteran vehicles should be allowed to use the roads though they did not fully comply with the new regulations. Although veteran cars built before 1915 enjoy some exemptions under the regulations, these did not apply to cars which had never been registered under the 1903 Motor Car Act. This, of course, included cars built before that date and never used on the road or vehicles subsequently imported into the country.

One of the key factors in this decision was that the 1894 Bremer car, the oldest four-wheeled British built motor car, which was restored at that time was refused registration because it did not comply with the 1963 construction and use regulations. This was hardly surprising, as it had been in the Walthamstow museum for over 40 years at that time. It had never been registered under the 1903 act because its constructor, Frederick Bremer of Walthamstow, had always tested it at night to avoid police prosecution and had laid it up in his shed before the Motor Car Act came into force. The crucial thing about these exemptions was that they defined a veteran car as one having been built before January 1 1905. Such vehicles were exempted from the requirements relating to speedometers, diameter of wheels, certain braking provisions and the need to be equipped with mudguards. Before vehicles were allowed to take advantage of these concessions, the owner had to obtain a certificate confirming that the car was constructed before 1905 from the officer in charge of the National Collection of Road Transport at London's Science Museum. The Minister of Transport—at that time surely the much maligned Ernest Marples—believed that these concessions were unlikely to inconvenience other road users in view of the low speed of these vehicles, their extremely limited numbers, and the small use to which they are likely to be put.

The difficulty of defining precisely the veteran period is that the pace of technological advance was so rapid in those days; it seems impossible to credit that the 1899 belt-driven, rear-engined Daimler and the 1903 60 hp Mercedes emanated from the same factory. There is as much difference in conception between the two vehicles as there is between a Wright biplane and a Spitfire. After that first frenzied advance in development, the pace slowed down. By the outbreak of the First World War, just about every technical feature which has been used on motor cars built since that time had been introduced, though contemporary technology and metallurgy could not always cope with advanced concepts. There is still a great deal of research to be done on such innovations, incidentally; for example it is still difficult to determine when the first use was made of forced induction on a road-going car to increase its power: a reference in the 1910 Paris Show report of *The Autocar* refers to a primitive supercharger called the Decupli which was tested on a 12/15 hp Mors car and gave encouraging results. However, earlier references, couched in the appallingly obscure technical prose adopted by journalists who could not understand the workings of the motor car but wished to cloak their ignorance in pomposity, appeared to indicate that some sort of supercharger was in fact used by at least one engine manufacturer in the late 1890s! And the American Chadwick company certainly used blowers for competition work from 1906 and may have fitted them to some production cars.

The discussion of technical advances is also germane to the dating of vehicles. It can be crucial to know when a particular technological development occurred to be able to establish the authenticity of a vehicle; for instance, although electric lighting was available for motor cars from the very early days, it was unreliable, and consequently only a few brave pioneers experimented with it, the rest preferring to put their trust in acetylene headlamps and oil side lamps, which could generally be trusted to stay alight for the duration of a journey. It was not until C.F. Kettering, of the Dayton Electrical Laboratories Company (better known by their acronym of 'Delco') devised a reliable electric starting and lighting dynamo installation for Cadillac, that the use of electric lamps on motor cars became general. So, given a specific vehicle, one can instantly see whether its equipment is appropriate by reference to contemporary advertisements for accessories.

However, for more precise dating, one has to combine not only a sound technological knowledge with a nose for what is right, but one must also be prepared to undertake considerable detective work. Dating some cars can prove to be simplicity itself; for instance, though the Model T Ford was made in such huge numbers, careful records were kept of engine numbers and styling differences (such as they were) so that there exists considerable documentation on the model. Given the engineering details and the engine and chassis number (which should in most cases be identical) it is possible to date a Model T almost to the day. The only difficulty can arise in the case of a car which has been reconstructed at some time of its life—or indeed, fabricated from spare parts in recent years. Other marques and models are as well documented—especially in America, where enthusiasts produce fat books which detail every distinguishing mark of certain popular antique vehicles. The American fashion for totally authentic restorations (although one can question authenticity which results in a vehicle looking better than it did when new) is thus served to the full.

There are ways of dating more obscure makes, though these are more time-consuming. The engine numbers of many early cars were recorded in various publications intended to help the insurance industries in the 1920s and 1930s. In France, *Le Catalogue des Catalogues* listed virtually every car sold in France between about 1905 and the date of publication, often going into great detail on engine numbers, differences between various models and the location of their manufacturers. A similar publication produced in England was the *Motor Car Index*, which again chronicles models by the most obscure makers, and gives engine numbers where available. However, some manufacturers still played 'hard to get', refusing to divulge engine numbers in case they revealed the paucity of their production to their commercial rivals. Other manufacturers, seeking to impress, applied the reverse tactics, and fabricated series of engine numbers which on the surface indicated vast production runs, but which in fact meant very little. So, if it is impossible to find the date from the engine number, one must resort to other methods. Research will show over what period a particular model of car was produced. Given that, one needs details of annual model changes, which were normally covered by the motoring press. If this information is available, it must then be sifted carefully to see whether any mechanical peculiarities appeared to differentiate one year from the next.

For instance, the Edwardian car I am currently restoring, a 16/20 hp Pilain, built in Lyons, can be dated before the 1911 Paris Salon for the simple reason that at that time the company switched from using a Zenith carburettor, modified to their own requirements, to a Solex. Equally, at the same period, they changed the method of operation of the gearbox from using two selection rods from the gear lever to having only one, which moved both fore and aft and radially. Then, knowing when the peculiar final drive system of the earlier models (which had double crown wheels and pinions as well as half shafts ending in gears to drive the hubs) went out of production, it is possible to pinpoint the construction date of the vehicle pretty closely, even without having any list which details engine and chassis numbers.

A remarkable resurrection of a most historic early car took place in 1979-80, when Alan 'Bob' Chamberlain recreated the 1904 racing 90 hp Napier L48 Samson, one of the most visually exciting of the early racing cars, with a pointed bonnet whose sides were formed up of the cooling tubes of the radiator. The Samson had been broken up many years before, and its 20-litre engines used to power a boat; Mr Chamberlain using original drawings completely rebuilt the chassis to the original specifications, creating a problem for those who seek to date old cars, for while the car was 1904 in specification and construction it had actually been built at the end of the 1970s. But in view of the fact that at least one replica veteran car built in the 1960s has in all innocence been dated as being constructed in the late 1890s by the Veteran Car Club it would seem churlish to deny this excellent recreation the honour due to it.

Tracing the history of a car

Anyone who owns an early motor car is naturally interested in its history. It used to be easy to trace the previous owners of an early car. In Britain the starting point always used to be the log book issued to every registered motor car following the 1920 motor car act. This listed all previous owners, their changes of address and full and accurate specifications of the car. But since the central licencing records in Britain became computerised in the late 70s, things seem to be a little more difficult.

Now the computer only keeps limited records, and details of owners, before the car was placed on the computer file, have been discarded. Owners who demanded their old log books back were usually satisfied, though it was often found that the earlier log books, which contained much valuable information, had been summarily destroyed.

Also, the computer vehicle details were often inaccurate. In many cases, early cars were listed in their log books by their taxable horsepower, which was based on the dimensions of the cylinder bore only, ignoring the stroke. The government employees who transferred the details from the old log books to the computer worked from tables giving the cylinder bore, but used their own initiative to determine the stroke, thereby invariably arriving at a completely erroneous swept volume for the engine, due to the radical changes in engine design over the past 40 or 50 years. So, if the log book (or rather 'vehicle registration document') as nowadays issued proves unhelpful, one can always turn detective to search out a vehicle's origin. For example, does the dashboard of your car bear a dealer's identification plate? If so, is that dealer still in business? If he is one of the older, smaller motor dealers, who has not been prevailed upon to streamline his operations, it is possible that he may still retain his old sales ledgers. He may, indeed, even remember your car. This was true in the case of the 1927 Clyno car which I have owned since 1961.

Though I had a log book with the car when I bought it, it dated from 1939, and the licencing authorities had no details of the car's original owner. But when I began to restore the vehicle, and stripped off the door trim, I found among the curious miscellany of items (including a pair of vintage underpants!) which had slipped past the door frame and into the inner recesses of the lower door, a small ebonite plate with the name of a motor dealer in Tenbury Wells, not far from Hereford. The dealer's name was certainly unusual—'G.E.T.H. Maund'—and the company still seemed to be in existence, though a letter failed to evoke any response. But a little while afterwards I drove down to Tenbury Wells, and found that Mr Maund was definitely still in business, in a small but rambling garage entered through a timbered archway that must have once served a stables. Mr Maund, a small elderly man, certainly had his sales ledgers going back 50 years, but could find no trace of my car. However, one thing which had been puzzling me was that the car bore a West Riding of Yorkshire index mark, which seemed incongruous for a dealership several hundred miles removed. I mentioned this to Mr Maund, and at once his face brightened.

'Oh, yes. I do remember that Clyno', he nodded. 'It originally belonged to my wife's second cousin, William Hayward, who was a big fruit and vegetable merchant in Blackpool. He used to drive it from Blackpool to Covent Garden Market every week and go home laden with produce. He died in 1937, and as my wife was the only relative, he left her the Clyno and a 1910 Model T Ford. I broke the Ford for scrap, but sold the Clyno after a few months to Bert Newell, a local man. He drove it through the war and then sold it himself.' There was

Where did old racing cars go to after their careers ended? This 1908 Grand Prix Mercedes, similar to that year's winning car, found its way to America, where it was still racing in 1914, here in the Santa Monica (California) Grand Prize Race. This could be the car discovered in the late 1930s in a shed on the Benington, Vermont, estate of Karl H. Martin, designer of the super-luxury Wasp automobile of the early 1920s, and still extant today. The wrecked car is a 1913 GP Sunbeam.

the missing link. The log book which I had began with Mr Newell, whose name I had not mentioned to Mr Maund.

With earlier, perhaps more historic vehicles, there is always a sporting chance that the vehicle may have been illustrated in the motoring press of its day. In such a case, there is no substitute for industry. The index which some of the early motoring magazines issued annually is not always to be trusted, and in any case cannot be comprehensive enough to list vehicles caught by chance in a photograph. You may also find correspondence in the magazine from the car's owner mentioning his vehicle. And there is always a lucky chance that you may come across a photograph in some modern publication which throws some light on the origins of your vehicle.

Some years ago I wrote an article on the early days of Aston Martin, and included in the photographs, provided by a former employee of the company, was one of a car which had once belonged to a Captain J.C. Douglas, which had apparently been written off by colliding with a street bollard after a late night party. The cast aluminium number plate had been smashed in the collision, but the central portion remained legible. The article was read by an enthusiast who had an early Aston Martin tourer with an obscure history, and sure enough the central digits of the registration were the same as that in the crashed car. He therefore wrote to the man who had provided the photograph, who was able to corroborate that the car had indeed been rebuilt after the accident and that was why this particular vehicle had a number of non-standard features.

The first British car registrations

Registration of motor vehicles became compulsory in Britain in 1904, at which time the general speed limit was raised from 12 to 20 mph. Initially, registrations were issued to owners rather than vehicles: this list records known owners of Number 1 issued in 1904 in each registration district. The premier English number, A1, was issued to Earl Russell; Scotland's premier number, S1, went to that great motoring enthusiast, Sir J.H.A. MacDonald, the Lord Justice Clerk, who had been interested in horseless carriages since the mid-1890s, and who later became Lord Kingsburgh.

A-1   (London) Earl Russell
AB-1 (Worcestershire) Lieutenant-Colonel Walker, Worcester
AC-1 (Warwickshire) H.G. Hawkes, Leamington Spa
AD-1 (Gloucestershire) Dr H.P. Fernald, Cheltenham
AF-1 (Cornwall) W.J. Powell, St Columb
AL-1 (Nottinghamshire) R.U. Knowles, Nottingham
AN-1 (West Ham) C.E. Scrutton
AR-1 (Hertfordshire) Lord Brownlow, Berkhamsted
AW-1 (Shropshire) W.H. Foster, Newport
BA-1 (Salford) F.W. Wheatcroft
BB-1 (Newcastle-upon-Tyne) W. Dunn
BD-1 (Northamptonshire) A. Smith, Thrapston
BF-1 (Dorset) Colonel J.R.P. Goodden, Sherborne
BH-1 (Buckinghamshire) T. Mosley, Uxbridge
BJ-1 (East Suffolk) R.J. Major, Carthew
BK-1 (Portsmouth) T.S. Foster, Southsea
BL-1 (Berkshire) Captain F.C. Loder-Symonds, Faringdon

BM-1 (Bedfordshire) The Duke of Bedford
BU-1 (Oldham) T. Crossman, Oldham
BW-1 (Oxfordshire) E.J. Bevers, Oxford
BX-1 (Carmarthenshire) G. Evans, Llanelli
BY-1 (Croydon) E.A. Preston
CB-1 (Blackburn) G.H. Woods
CC-1 (Caernarvonshire) L.W. Jelf-Petit, Llanwrst
CD-1 (Brighton) F.H. Nye, Worthing
CM-1 (Birkenhead) Dr T.S. Floyd
CN-1 (Gateshead) H. Eastcott
CP-1 (Halifax) Dr Wright
CR-1 (Southampton) R.E. Lauder
CW-1 (Burnley) Thomas Gott Parkinson
CX-1 (Huddersfield) F.W. Mills
CY-1 (Swansea) A.L. Lewis
DA-1 (Wolverhampton) S.R. Rhodes
DK-1 (Rochdale) R. Walker
DP-1 (Reading) W.H. Greenhough
DS-1 (Peebles) Sir D.F. Hay
DU-1 (Coventry) C.K. Welsh
DW-1 (Newport, Monmouthshire) G.L. Watson
DX-1 (Ipswich) H.G. Kettle
DY-1 (Hastings) J.F. Mastin
EC-1 (Westmorland) C.W. Wilson, Kirkby Lonsdale
ED-1 (Warrington) E. Woods
EE-1 (Grimsby) T.G. Tickler
EI-1 (Sligo) R. Simpson
EJ-1 (Cardiganshire) E.F. Szumper, London
EK-1 (Wigan) E.R. Crippin
EL-1 (Bournemouth) H. Newlyn
EO-1 (Barrow-in-Furness) J. Fisher
ET-1 (Rotherham) B.H. Pickford
EW-1 (Huntingdonshire) The Earl of Sandwich, Huntingdon
EX-1 (Great Yarmouth) H. Chamberlain
F-1 (Essex) P.J. Sheldon, Chelmsford
FA-1 (Burton-upon-Trent) G.F. Reading
FN-1 (Canterbury) Dr A. Pearce
FP-1 (Rutland) Captain W.J. Roberts, Dudley
G-1 (Glasgow) R.J. Smith
HS-1 (Renfrew) W. Todd
IK-1 (Dublin County) T.S. Plunkett, Baldoyle
IN-1 (Kerry) W.J. Girvan
IO-1 (Kildare) P.T. Somerville-Large
IU-1 (Limerick) Captain J.S. Lyons
JI-1 (Tyrone) Colonel H. Irvine, Omagh
K-1 (Liverpool) A.G. Lyster
KI-1 (Waterford) Marquis of Waterford
KS-1 (Roxburgh) Dr W. Blair, Jedburgh
LI-1 (West Meath) L.C. James, Mullingar
LS-1 (Selkirk) Dr J.B. Ronaldson, Haddington

M-1   (Chester) M. Egerton, Knutsford
MI-1   (Wexford) Colonel J.R. Magrath
N-1   (Manchester) W. Kay, Stretford
OS-1   (Wigtown) M. Fox
P-1   (Surrey) F.G. Howell, Oxshott
RS-1   (Aberdeen) R.S. Jackson
S-1   (Edinburgh) Right Honourable Sir J.H.A. Macdonald
SA-1   (Aberdeenshire) D.A. Ramsay, Dyce
SB-1   (Argyll) J.S. Mathew, Dunoon
SH-1   (Berwick) Sir G.H. Boswell
SJ-1   (Bute) Right Honourable G.A. Murray
SR-1   (Forfar) A.M. White
SU-1   (Kincardineshire) A.G. Ogston, Aberdeen
SY-1   (Midlothian) J.A. Maconochie
TS-1   (Dundee) A. Watt
U-1   (Leeds) A.C. Briggs
UI-1   (Borough of Londonderry) M.A. Robinson
V-1   (Lanark) Captain H.S. Streatfield, Sunderland
W-1   (Sheffield) S.E. Fedon
WS-1   (Leith) G.W. Mackie

At least one of the vehicles in this list still exists with its original number (M-1), and in its original location (Tatton Park, Knutsford, Cheshire). It is a 1900 Benz 3½ hp 'Comfortable' originally owned by the Honourable Maurice Egerton of Tatton Park, which became the property of the National Trust on his death. The National Trust has restored the car, which is displayed alongside an electric town car of later vintage.

In the above list, it is apparent that initially registrations containing the letter 'I' referred to Irish authorities, while the inclusion of the letter 'S' denoted a Scottish registration, though Lanark was an exception to this rule.

3 The Artefacts

Ford archives

I know how Howard Carter felt when he opened Tutankhamen's tomb. For I was there when the buried treasure of Dagenham was unearthed. Just after the last war, when storage was at a premium, Ford of Dagenham decided that their dead files were too valuable to scrap, but took up too much office space. So they hit on the bright idea of walling up the files beneath the engine building, the original Dagenham Ford plant. It was not until the mid 1970s that the hidden cache of papers was rediscovered, when the walls were knocked down to install some piping. Some of the files had been taken away for scrap, but an alert security man, realising that the files might have some historic value, contacted me and told me that he felt that more existed that was worth saving. So, accompanied by Ford's Company Secretary, I went down to Dagenham to see what had been discovered. The old engine building is founded on concrete piles, which extend deep down into the Thameside marsh. When you go below floor level, you can see the tops of the piles on which the entire building stands, as though on stilts. Between the piles, brick walls had been erected, and it was behind these that the files had been discovered.

We had to scramble up a makeshift ladder through a gap in the brickwork, and there an amazing sight met our eyes. There were racks and racks of steel boxes full of files, some still in position, some having fallen on to the floor as the shelving had collapsed under their weight. The floor, thick with harsh dust, was littered with paper, an indiscriminate jumble of old payslips, files, leaflets and advertisements. I picked up a tattered piece of paper which I noticed because of the bright red and blue colouring on it. I opened it out—it was the middle third of a poster advertising an open day at Ford's Antwerp plant in the mid 1930s. I knew then that the files were likely to have some historic significance. Just how much significance was only to become apparent as I began delving through the rusty tin boxes. I pulled out a folder. Pasted to it was a slip which said, 'Mr Henry Ford 1929'. It was full of correspondence from Henry Ford—or at least his office, for Ford rarely signed letters himself—and related to the purchase of items for the huge museum that Ford was then establishing at Greenfield Village, near his Dearborn plant. Ford had commissioned an Englishman named Morton to 'spend me ten million dollars', and here were some of the instructions as to what Morton was to buy with that collosal sum. There was a listing of various types of early steam engine, either items that Morton had discovered or particular types which Ford felt that his

Above *During the period 1928-38 Ford of Britain organised its own motor shows, usually at London's Albert Hall. This archive photograph is of the 1937 exhibition.*

Above right *An official car park sticker from the 1937 Ford Show at the Albert Hall.* **Right** *Admission tickets are among the rarer motoring ephemera. These are two of a series of tickets issued for the 1937 Ford Exhibition in the Albert Hall.* **Below right** *Some of the historic documents discovered walled up at Ford's Dagenham plant; these items relate to the opening of the Cologne Ford plant in 1931.*

collection needed. There were instructions on buying two Cotswold cottages which were to be re-erected in the United States, complete with the soil from their gardens. There were orders for china and other domestic items for Mr Ford, and of course there was the routine correspondence one would expect from a motor magnate who was at that time in the process of greatly enlarging his empire.

However, the correspondence from Henry Ford was only a very small part of what was there. As I searched through the assorted files it became apparent that here was a unique treasure trove of correspondence relating to the setting up and administration of Ford's European Empire in the 1930s. These were the personal files of Sir Percival Perry, founder of the Ford operation in Britain, and one of the pioneers of the British motor industry. Perry, a close personal friend of Henry Ford, had started in the motor trade in 1898, selling accessories and components for the horseless carriages of the day and had been present when the first two Ford cars to reach Britain had been uncrated sometime at the end of 1903. He had been associated with the business run by their importer, one Aubrey Blakiston, who operated an unsuccessful firm called the American Motor Car Agency. Perry, realising the potential of the Ford vehicles, had taken over the agency when Blakiston failed, renamed it the Central Motor Car Company and built it up into the foundation of Ford's operations in Britain. When Henry Ford decided to set up a branch company in England in 1909, he asked Perry to head it. Perry had broken with Ford in 1919, over a matter of dealer policy, and had helped to set up the Slough Trading Estate. Then,

deciding to go into retirement, he had taken the lease of the Channel Island of Herm and retired from business.

However, in 1928 Henry Ford decided to revitalise his entire manufacturing operation. The immortal Ford Model T, of which over 16.5 million had been built, had just gone out of production and Ford was getting under way with the new Model A. He needed a man of exceptional ability to head his European operations, and to take charge of the gigantic new plant which was to be built beside the Thames at Dagenham. Visiting England early in 1928, and travelling incognito as 'Mr Robinson', Henry Ford had tea with the King and Queen at Cliveden, lunched with Lloyd George in the Houses of Parliament and spoke to a great assembly of British Motor Trade dignitaries.

Having decided that a partnership with Sir Herbert Austin to build cars for Britain had no future in it, Ford decided to offer Percival Perry the job of building up a European Ford industry and consequently, shortly before he sailed for home, Ford telegraphed Perry to meet him on the ship at Southampton. Perry, who had kept closely in touch with the fortunes of Ford Motor Company during the period since his resignation, accepted Ford's offer eagerly, bubbling over with ideas for the new organisation. And here, in the dust and dark beneath the throbbing engine plant, was the record of how Percival Perry had set about his unprecedented task.

Sorting through this huge pile of material—there were over 100 boxes, and a large truck was needed to transport them—was an immense task. The amount of material filed was a monument to the industry (some of it possibly a little misplaced) of Perry's secretarial staff, especially his personal secretary Miss Vera Howard, who was with him all the time that he headed Ford in Britain. There were literally hundreds of memoranda annotated in that green pencil which only Percival Perry was allowed to use in the Ford empire. There were telegrams by the dozen. In those days, everything seems to have been committed to paper. Indeed, many inter-office memoranda carried the printed message 'Verbal messages don't go'.

Much of the material which had been saved was dross. There were written acknowledgements of letters, orders for vehicle components and machine tools which spread to several pages of close set typing, yet which were totally meaningless. Amazingly, some of the material was as fresh as the day it had been put in those files over 40 years earlier. Other items had been attacked by damp, or by rats and were beyond saving. But to sift through the day to day correspondence of people who had hitherto been merely two dimensional names in a history book, brought them alive in a way that one would have thought impossible. There, for example, typed in the blue ink that signified the correspondence of Ford France, were details of Henry Ford's stormy relationship with Emile Mahis, when the two manufacturers formed a liaison to produce Ford V8 cars under the name *Matford* in Mathis' Strasbourg factory. Ford needed more factory space, since his plant at Asnières, near Paris, was too small to meet demand; Mathis needed finance. But the two men were such rugged individualists that the liaison was doomed from the start, and broke apart shortly before the outbreak of the Second World War. Here were the agreements, the acrimonious correspondence, the efforts of the chief of Ford France, Maurice Dollfuss, a rugby-playing giant, who seemed a little out of his league as he strove to keep the peace between Henry and Emile.

There were other sidelights on motoring history, like invitations to cinema shows of long ago, a telegram announcing the construction of the first car at Ford's new Cologne factory in 1931. There were posters, their bright colours unspoiled by their years of storage for the new V8, for the Ford truck and for the Ford car wireless set, on which you could hear the music of Fred Waring and his Pennsylvanians, sponsored by the Ford Motor Company. In all the years I have been associated with motor cars, I do not think anything has given me as much of a thrill of discovery as sorting through the lost treasure of Dagenham.

The first motoring magazine

The first automobile journal appeared as long ago as October 1832, and was known as the *Journal of Elemental Locomotion and of Advantages Resulting from the application of Steam and other Power as connected with Arts, Sciences, Manufacturers, Commerce & Agriculture, Reporter of all Projects of Inventions, Discoveries, Patents, etc, etc, of National Utility*. It was edited by Alexander Gordon whose father, David, had in 1822 patented a curious three-wheeled steam carriage in which the motive power was furnished by a small railway engine running inside a drum some nine feet in diameter and urging the machine forward like a squirrel in a cage. Gordon senior had also patented, in 1824, a carriage propelled by six hollow iron legs designed to give the mechanical effect of horses' feet, as he did not believe that smooth wheels would be sufficient to propel a carriage.

The younger Gordon, who had already written a book entitled *A Treatise on Elemental Locomotion*, was a civil engineer and his journal was published with the aim of 'showing the utility—commercially, politically and morally—of introducing steam carriages into general practice upon the highways of the kingdom, and how the knowledge and practice of mechanical science had brought this desideratum within our power'. The *Journal of Elemental*

The Journal of Elemental Locomotion *was the first 'motor magazine'. Only six issues were produced in 1832-3* (Foulkes-Halbard Collection).

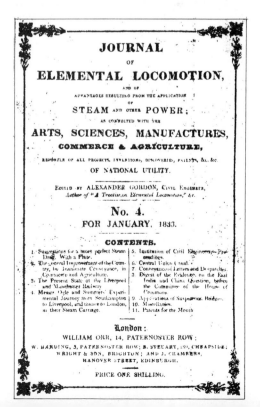

Locomotion was published by William Orr of 14, Paternoster Row, London, and sold for one shilling.

Gordon saw the steam carriage as being the potential bringer of great social reform. In the first issue, he wrote: 'Supposing that steam carriages should be employed in conveying passengers only and the whole change to be effected in a sudden manner. I think there would in the first instance be a diminished demand for agricultural produce, but the following process would take place. As the demand for agricultural produce was diminished, the price of such produce would fall, food would become cheaper and the cheapness of food would benefit partly the labouring class and partly the capitalists, the one obtaining higher real wages and the other higher profits. This increase in real wages and in profits would effect a great encouragement to manufacturing industry and necessarily lead to an increase in the manufacturing population and in the amount of capital employed in manufacture . . . .

'The adoption of steam coaches will set trade free from its great commercial difficulty because they can be laid up and kept idle without considerable loss and brought out again when wanted, without any new outlay; also fuel does not fluctuate either in price or quality, to any considerable extent, like horse corn. In short, the capital embarked on a steam-coach trade will not be so rapidly wasted as at present in horses. Owing to the great number of horses which must first be bought and then kept to do the same work as one steam coach, the first outlay in stock will be very small in steam coaches compared with horses; the same of stables, ostlers and harnesses . . . .

'In viewing the moral advantages which must result from steam carriages, we find them of no less importance . . . Acceleration in the speed of travelling, if unaccompanied by danger, is eagerly sought after because the period of discomfort is lessened. But steam carriages will not only lessen the discomfort by shortening its duration; they can be so equipped that positive comfort—nay, luxury—may be enjoyed. A steam carriage is perfectly under control and consequently much more safe than horses. The life of a traveller cannot be jeopardised by the breaking of a rein, horses being frightened, running off, etc, etc; the steamer, the honourable committee report to the house (1831), "is perfectly safe for passengers"'.

The *Journal* was highly critical of railways, because of the high maintenance costs of the locomotives and track, and advocated steam carriages on common roads as the best system of locomotion.

Reports covered the leading steam carriage developments of the day; in the second issue was a report of a trip made to Brighton in October 1832 by Walter Hancock's steam carriage *Infant*, the first self-propelled vehicle to make this traditional journey. (There was, incidentally, a plan afoot in the 1970s to construct a replica of a Hancock steam carriage, which seems to have foundered for lack of finance; it would have been nice to have seen such a primitive machine running alongside the veteran cars in the annual Brighton Run!) In the fourth issue the *Journal* gave Gordon's suggestions 'for a more perfect steam drag', a light four-wheeled carriage which combined all the best features of currently available vehicles and which looked remarkably like some of the experimental motor cars of the 1870s and 1880s. That issue also carried details of 'Messrs Ogle & Summers' experimental journey from Southampton to Liverpool, and thence to London in their steam carriage'.

The sixth issue carried what amounted to a road test, describing a run on

Hancock's latest steam omnibus from the Hancock factory at Stratford, Essex, to a firm of coachbuilders in Islington, where it was to be painted and trimmed before going into service between Paddington and the City. That issue also carried news of the formation of the first motor club, 'a meeting of Noblemen and Gentlemen to promote the formation of a Society for the Amelioration of the Distress of the Country by means of Steam Transport and Agriculture', which had been organised on April 23 1833 by Gordon. An impressive provisional committee of noblemen and MPs was set up to form the association, which apparently was known as the Institution of Locomotion, but which does not seem to have achieved a great deal. It was, however, instrumental in producing a successor to the *Journal of Elemental Locomotion*, the *Journal of Steam Transport and Husbandry*, which appeared in 1834 and possibly only survived for one issue. Like its predecessor, the *Journal of Steam Transport* was highly critical of the railways, its main article being entitled: 'Railroad Impositions Detected; or Facts and Arguments to Prove that Railroads can never compete effectually with canals, steam carriages on common roads or even stage coaches'.

A set of the *Journal of Elemental Locomotion* was apparently preserved by the Institution of Mechanical Engineers, but seems to have disappeared in recent years.

The first British motoring magazines

It was in 1895 that a British magazine first began to pay attention to the new sport of motoring. In the early summer of 1895, Harry J. Lawson, the entrepreneur who is either credited with having founded the British motor industry or with having conned gullible investors out of many thousands of pounds for his over-capitalised companies, approached Edmund Dangerfield, the 31-year-old editor of *Cycling*, founded in 1891. 'Dangerfield', enthused Lawson, 'this is your great opportunity. I want you to get in on the ground floor by starting an automobile journal before anyone else seizes this golden chance.' Lawson, it seems, was looking for a journal that would be the mouthpiece of his company; though Dangerfield did not take up Lawson's offer to found a motoring journal at that time, he began to incorporate motoring matters into the editorial text of *Cycling*.

When in 1895 the Mayor of Tunbridge Wells, Sir David Salomons, organised a small exhibit of self-propelled vehicles, Dangerfield wrote in the edition of October 26 that the production of automobiles presented 'great opportunity for the cycle trade to extend its scope'. 'By the way', Dangerfield continued, 'there seems a great diversity in naming the new vehicles and some generic name is needed. WHAT ABOUT MOTORCAR!' Within a week of the publication of those words, the first British magazine entirely devoted to motor cars appeared, published by Iliffes, proprietors of two cycling papers. Their magazine, *The Autocar*, first appeared on November 2 1895, edited by J.J. Henry Sturmey, who, when he left motoring journalism, took up the manufacture of Durreyea motor cars in a factory at Widdrington, Coventry.

In its opening number, *The Autocar* explained its choice of a title, 'Horseless Carriage—Automobile Carriage—Automatic Carriage—Autocar. All these names have been used to designate the latest production of the ingenuity of man, the motor driven road carriage, irrespective of whether steam, electricity, hot-air or petroleum be the motive power. The last is the latest. The latest is the best, and, as 'the best is good enough for us'—as our American cousins have it—its adoption to indicate the journal as well as the machine in those interests it is published scarcely needs explanation. Nor is excuse needed for our entry into the world of periodic literature. Every new movement is fostered and encouraged by publicity and the free letting in upon it of the light of public opinion. The power of the press of this country as an educator and a moulder of sentiment is unparalled, but the general and even the technical press has too vast a field of labour to devote to any one movement that amount of attention which it requires, and consequently the specialist press not only finds a reason for existence but becomes a necessity where any new and important principles are involved . . . If by the dissemination of knowledge upon the subject generally, and the discussion of designs and principles, *The Autocar* can assist, our pages will ever be freely placed at the disposal of the public.'

At first, *The Autocar* was fairly closely allied with the dubious business ventures of Harry J. Lawson, who was trying to establish a monopoly on the British motor industry by buying up all the leading continental patents and floating over-capitalised companies to build vehicles using these patents for the British market. But it soon became an independent and highly respected voice, and today is the oldest motoring magazine of all. A year and three weeks after its foundation *The Autocar* recorded 'A red letter day', November 14 1896, the day on which the 1878 Locomotives on Highways Act was withdrawn in favour of the Light Road Locomotives Act. This raised the permitted speed limit for horseless carriages to 12 mph, instead of the 2 mph in towns and 4 mph in the country decreed by the former act. To celebrate the event, *The Autocar* that day was printed in red.

By that time, *The Autocar* had a rival. On October 15 1896, the *Automotor and Horseless Vehicle Journal* had made its bow. Edited by Stanley Spooner, the *Automotor Journal* was for many years distinguished by its yellow cover. Spooner was later to be assisted by Edgar N. Duffield, whose quirky style of writing was quite distinct from any of his contemporaries. A personal friend of Alfred Harmsworth (himself a pioneer motorist), Duffield also edited the *Ford Times*, which was launched in 1912 by his friend, Percival Perry, in charge of the Ford interests in Britain. Duffield also edited an ephemeral magazine of the Great War called *The King's Highway*. Incidentally, Stanley Spooner edited *Automotor Journal* for well over 20 years before he learned to drive; it was only in the mid 1920s that Duffield finally persuaded Spooner to buy an Austin Heavy 12 and learn to handle it. Like his contemporary, Charles Gray of *The Aeroplane*, Spooner felt that lack of experience of the subject he was writing about actually heightened his critical faculties.

In October 1898 Charles Cordingly, a rumbustious character, who ran the annual laundry exhibition in the Agricultural Hall, Islington, launched *The Motor Car Journal*, with a cover price of only one penny compared with the three pence charged by its two rivals. Then, in its issue of November 11 1899, Edmund Dangerfield's *Cycling* changed its name to *Cycling and Motoring* and announced a special motor supplement would be included in the December 9 number. This was a prolific period for the launch of motoring magazines. In October 1899 the *Scottish Motor World*, a monthly magazine, was introduced, while in November 1899, the Automobile Club of Great Britain and Northern Ireland brought out its own *Journal*. In February 1900 the Irish cycling journalist R.J. Mecredy launched *Motor News*.

Left *The Gordon Crosby illustration on the cover of this 1922* The Autocar *was sold in the 1920s by the magazine's proprietors, Iliffe & Son, for ten guineas. It is now in a private collection in France.*

Right *A 1904 copy of* The International Motor Review, *an English language magazine published in Paris.*

February 12 1902 saw the launch of a new magazine by Edmund Dangerfield. Priced at one penny, it was called *Motor Cycling and Motoring*. Though its title emphasised motorcycling its contents were principally aimed at motorists. Yet another magazine appeared on March 8 1902; this was *Motoring Illustrated*, a threepenny publication produced by the Dublin journalists, Noel and Edward Kenealey. Shortly afterwards, the Honourable John Scott-Montagu (afterwards the first Lord Montagu of Beaulieu) brought out an up-market weekly priced at sixpence, called *Car Illustrated*. This was very much a society magazine, with something of the tone of its contemporary *Country Life* (which also launched a motoring supplement around that time, covering the week's motoring news in high quality text and illustrations). Alongside *Car Illustrated*, Scott-Montagu launched a tabloid monthly, the *Motor Car Magazine* in 1903, but it only ran for a couple of years, while *The Car* (which was ultimately rechristened *Car and Golf*) survived into the mid-1920s.

Another titled motor magazine editor was Viscount Massereene and Ferrard, who ran the *Automobile Owner and Steam and Electric Car Review*, which first appeared in 1906. The first trade paper appeared in October 1902, under the title *Automobile and Carriage Builders Journal*. Despite the rapid growth in the number of magazines produced, it was noted that when *Motor Cycling* changed

Left *A 1930 copy of* The Motor *with a splendid cover by Bryan de Grineau.*
Right *Founded in 1912,* The Light Car and Cyclecar *pioneered the use of a photographic cover. Featured on this 1923 edition is the young Raymond Mays.*

its title to *The Motor* on January 21 1903, there were a mere 8,465 private motorists in Britain. Interestingly enough, the first issue of *The Motor* had a circulation of 25,000, said to be 'Equal to that of any other for Motor papers', a figure which had risen to 35,874 by September 30 1903. The year 1905 saw the launch of yet another motoring magazine, *Motor Trader*; the need for such a magazine was shown by the fact that by 1907 the number of private car owners in Britain had risen to 32,451, yet a total of 34,000 people were employed in the construction and maintenance of motor vehicles in the country.

In 1909, Dangerfield reintroduced *Motor Cycling*, now devoted entirely to two wheeled motor vehicles. In November 1912 he launched a further magazine to respond to the growing phenomonen of small vehicles which were less refined than conventional cars yet more elaborate than motorcycles; the new magazine, edited by A.C. Armstrong, was called *The Cyclecar*, and its first number set up a record for its day for any specialised magazine by selling 100,000 after a hasty reprint. Then, inevitably, cyclecars became more elaborate and more akin to their larger brethren, and in 1916 *The Cyclecar* became the *Light Car and Cyclecar*, under which title it was to survive another 40 years. By 1914, some 74 motoring papers had been produced, including two dailies: *Daily Motoring Illustrated* (1905) and the *Daily Auto* (1908). The first survived eight days, the second only one . . ..

The first French motoring magazines

The first French magazine totally devoted to motor cars was *La Locomotion Automobile*, a monthly publication which appeared for the first time on December 1 1894. At that time, there can only have been a handful of cars on the road in France, yet the popularity of the magazine grew so that it was subsequently published twice a month and then weekly. The founding director of the magazine was Raoul Vuillemat. Exactly two months later, on February 1 1896, Paul Meyan brought out a weekly motoring paper *La France Automobile*; a less successful venture of that year was *L'Automobile Journal*, published in Lyon by a M Vitou. Only a few issues appeared. *Les Sports Modernes*, founded in 1898, featured motor cars in its pages and published some fine coloured plates of Panhards and Decauvilles. A satirical motoring paper, *L'Auto-Vélo*, was first issued on May 15 1897, finding much humour in the replacement of the horse by the motor car. In August that year a rival publication, *La Trompe* was brought out by Pierre Lafitte and Frantz Raichel. Despite a list of contributors of great distinction, *La Trompe* was absorbed by *L'Auto-Vélo* within three months and by the beginning of 1898 *L'Auto-Vélo* had also folded.

The name was to reappear in a totally different form shortly afterwards in reaction to an attack by the cycling paper *Le Vélo* (founded in 1892) on the speeds achieved in the Paris-Marseilles-Paris motor race of 1896, when the winning car, Mayade's Panhard, averaged 30 km/h. So, on October 16 1900, Henri Desgrange brought out *L'Auto-Vélo*, printed on yellow paper to contrast with the green paper of *Le Vélo*. *Le Vélo*'s editor, Pierre Giffard, was duly incensed and sued *L'Auto-Vélo* for the use of the word *'Vélo'* in the title. On January 8 1902 the commercial court of the Siene ordered *L'Auto-Vélo* to take the word *Vélo* out of the title—which, after a lapse of many months, they did. The matter came to a head in October 1902, when *L'Auto-Vélo* organised a hill-climb at Gaillon, with an entry of 158 cars and motorcycles. At the last minute, the local Prefect and Mayor arrived on the scene to prevent the meeting taking place. *L'Auto-Vélo* claimed that the official indictment was the work of Pierre Giffard, editor of the hated *Vélo*. Copies of *Le Vélo* were ceremonially burned, while disappointed spectators 'howled and hissed at the name of Giffard'.

L'Auto was to become a prime force in the promotion of motor racing in France, giving its name to a celebrated race for three-litre cars, the Coupe de *l'Auto* and its title, if nothing else, survives today in the daily French sporting newspaper *L'Equipe*. As for *Le Vélo*, its victory was a hollow one, for in the Autumn of 1904 *Le Vélo* began to be printed on white paper, a sign, claimed *L'Auto*, that it was sick unto death. And, in November 1904 *Le Vélo* disappeared to be replaced by a new publication *Le Journal de l'Automobile du Cyclisme et des Tous les Sports*, whose first issue appeared on November 18 1904, under the editorship of G. de Papploski, the last editor of *Le Vélo*. It was printed on rose-tinted paper, but its future was far from rosy and it disappeared soon after. So, too, did *Le Monde Sportive*, another daily paper with a motoring flavour which appeared in May 1903, printed on light blue paper.

Another motoring daily, *Les Sports*, appeared on December 1 1904, edited by one of the great French sporting journalists, George Prade. It seems to have been the successor to an illustrated magazine of the same name, which was certainly current at the time of Paris-Madrid. Publication lasted until the end of the first decade of the 20th century. There was a great growth in illustrated sporting papers around the turn of the century. *La Vie au Grand Air*, which first appeared in April 1898, was one of the stable of magazines founded by the redoubtable Pierre Lafitte, it covered all kinds of sports in its pages, but was especially noteworthy for its dramatic photographs usually reproduced to the full extent of its large pages, and often in the form of a double page spread. A rival publication, *La Revue Sportive*, only lasted from 1902 to 1903.

Baudry de Saunier, who was to become one of the great names in French motoring journalism, launched *La Locomotion* in October 1901. The name was changed to *La Vie Automobile* in September 1903; Baudry de Saunier left to found his famous magazine *Omnia* in 1906 and editorship was taken over by Pol Ravigaux. He was succeeded in 1909 by Charles Faroux, another of the great French motoring journalists. *La Pratique Automobile*, launched in 1904, shortly afterwards absorbed *La France Automobile*, which had been running eight years. A popular illustrated magazine of the time, *Automobile Illustré*, appeared in September 1904, aimed at the popularisation of motoring.

There were English language magazines published in France at that period, too. The *International Motor Review*, incorporating *Motoring in France*, was first published in Paris at the beginning of 1904. Edited by R.F. Collins, it was a useful publication which gave marque histories concentrating on personalities behind the cars as well as interesting sidelights on motoring social events. Another magazine published in English for expatriates living in France was *Automobilia* (founded in 1904), a more luxurious publication which featured some fine coloured art plates, by artists such as René Vincent.

The French were well provided with motoring magazines in the days before the Second World War; one estimate reckoned that between the appearance of H.O. Duncan's *Le Véloceman*, a cycling paper founded in 1885, and the outbreak of the Second World War, some 84 magazines had appeared which had a specialist interest in either motoring or cycling. Among them can be included such magazines as *Le Monde Automobile, L'Echo Automobile, La Voiturette, La Revue de L'Automobile, L'Automobiliste* (a name revived in

Edited by the famous journalist, Charles Faroux, La Vie Automobile *was one of the best and longest-lived French motoring magazines.*

recent years by a quality French magazine for antique vehicle enthusiasts), and *L'Année Automobile.*

Other early magazines

Other countries had their motoring journals: America boasted *Horseless Age* and *Motor Age,* while the *Cycle and Automobile Trade Journal* gave much background on obscure manufacturers which was not forthcoming elsewhere. Austro-Germany had *Allgemeine Automobil Zeitung,* Italy *L'Automobile* and *Rapiditas.*

Primary reference sources

Most museums have a reference library to which public access can be gained on application. The National Motor Museum at Beaulieu, for example, has a comprehensive library housed in its administrative building, which can be seen by researchers free of charge without their needing to pay admission to the museum. The Royal Automobile Club in London has a large library, while one of the finest collections in Britain belongs to the Veteran Car Club of Great Britain and is housed at its headquartes in Ashwell, Hertfordshire. This has grown over the past half century to include examples of early publications from all over the world and the facility of using this marvellous collection is well worth the modest price of associate membership of the Veteran Car Club, the premier old vehicle organisation in the world, founded in 1930.

The larger American museums also have collections of historic material. One of the leading libraries of automotive literature is the Automotive History Department of the Detroit Public Library, which grew from a single book written by John Henry Knight purchased in 1896. Because of its geographical location, Detroit library became the natural depository for motoring literature as the collection grew until in 1944 a special room was set aside for it and in 1953 the automobile collection became a separate division within the library because of its importance.

Letters and autographs

There is nothing more fascinating than coming across a letter from a motoring pioneer describing some facet of his experiences. It is doubly fascinating when the signature at the bottom of the letter is a well known one. For instance, I have come across a letter from Sir Malcolm Campbell apologising for his inability to speak at a public meeting because he had decided to go off on his futile hunt for pirate treasure in the Cocos Islands. Such things can still be found, usually in the dead files of older companies.

Of course, if one can discover the address of a surviving pioneer, one can always write to him; but ensuring that one only asks precise questions and includes the return postage. It is equally exciting to come across a signed copy of a book; around 1970 I discovered in a small bookshop (since pulled down to make way for an overpass) a first edition of Sir Henry Birkin's book *Full Throttle,* still in its original dust jacket. On the flyleaf was inscribed 'Tim Birkin 1933', an especially poignant date because that was the year that Birkin died of septicaemia on his return from the Tripoli Grand Prix.

Three or four years later, a rural bookshop yielded a copy of the Earl of Cottenham's *Sicilian Circuit* with a personal inscription to a friend from the Earl, while the seldom visited top shelf of a bookcase in a seaside bookshop

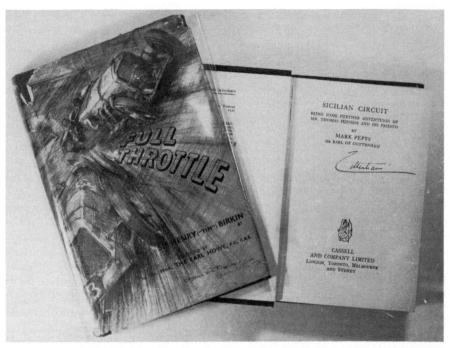

Two autographed motor racing books—Sir Henry Birkin's autobiographical Full Throttle, *with the original dust-jacket by Bryan de Grineau, and the Earl of Cottenham's novel* Sicilian Circuit. *Both date from the early 1930s.*

yielded a copy of *Fifty Years of Travel by Land, Water and Air*, by Frank Hedges Butler which had once been the personal property of the famous coach-builder H.J. Mulliner. There is always something intriguing in handling a book which has been through such famous hands.

Motoring novels

To the Victorian middle classes, the advent of the motor car ushered in an age of romance and freedom. Travel by railway had already become commonplace, and cycling—at least over any appreciable distance—was exclusively a male sport, despite the attentions of Mrs Amelia Bloomer. Now it was possible for both sexes to journey together, in delicious propinquity and a new age of freedom was ushered in, the more resourceful ladies actually began to drive motor cars; even 70 years later, something of the stir that was caused was conveyed by the hushed tone in which St John Nixon, a survivor of the 1900 Thousand Miles Trial, told me that Henry Hewetson, who imported Benz cars into Britain, 'Had given a Benz car to his friend Mrs Bazalgette, to drive in the event!' Unfortunately, photographs of the Trial reveal the good lady as being a somewhat forbidding amazon, and not the sylph-like creature the old man's description had conjured up.

Novelists, never slow to realise a promising market, were soon turning out romances based on the theme of man, woman and motor car, the earliest of such stories appearing around 1897. The first motoring novels—or rather novelettes—usually centred on the inability of the driver to stop his vehicle, and the consequence when the girl riding as passenger realised he had saved her life and expressed her gratitude with declarations of love. But early in the new century a motoring novel appeared which was to elevate the genre to a new height, gaining Royal patronage, and becoming something of a legend. The book was entitled *The Lightning Conductor*, and it was written by the husband and wife team of Charles and Alice Williamson. C.N. and A.M. Williamson went on to write dozens of books, all light romances, but none achieved success to match their first book, which was still being reprinted in the 1920s.

The plot of the *Lightning Conductor* was fairly simple; rich American heiress Molly Randolph, having bought a dreadful motor car called an Orient Express from a titled crook named Cecil-Lanstown, breaks down with it in France and is rescued by the driver of a Napier car. He is, in fact, the Honourable John Winston, son of Lady Brighthelmstone, but Miss Randolph mistakes him for the chauffeur. Winston, who had instantly fallen in love with Molly, goes along with this misconception and offers to act as chauffeur for her on her trip through France. Throughout the book, he manages to keep his emotions as tightly buttoned as his leather motoring jacket. Of course, in the end, he is recognised for who he is and the two are permitted, the conventions of society having been respected, to declare their love for each other.

What distinguished the *Lightning Conductor* from the earlier motoring novels was its authenticity; and this was hardly surprising because the Williamsons had based the main part of the book on their honeymoon. They had actually visited by motor car all the places described, and therefore the romantic plot was really only an overlay on an authentic travel book. However, they had not crossed France in a Napier like the hero and heroine of the book, but in the Orient Express which Charlie Williamson had bought to help him in his role as motoring correspondent of a motoring magazine called *The Traveller*. Indeed, several articles in that magazine were later expanded into episodes in the novel, a clear case of art imitating nature.

The *Lightning Conductor* opened the flood gates to a whole series of motoring novels, though in the case of the Williamsons the motoring content declined after 1910 or so, as Charlie Williamson's health deteriorated. He was the technical expert of the partnership, his wife the writer; after his death in

Many Edwardian motoring novels have attractive pictorial covers which capture the spirit of the age as much as their romantic storylines. Even King Edward VII read the motoring novels of C.N. and A.M. Williamson.

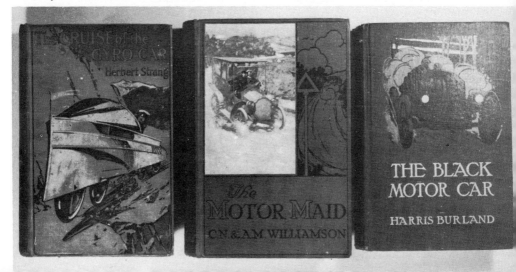

1916 she still continued to bring out books under the C.N. & A.M. Williamson name, claiming that he was still in communication with her from the spirit world! The last *Lightning Conductor* novel, *Return of the Lightning Conductor*, appeared in the 1930s. The Williamsons attracted many imitators, of whom Archibald Birt at least acknowledged his debt in a novel entitled *The Locust and the Ladybird* based on a motor tour through Australia in a Beeston Humber car.

Motoring novels are one of the growing areas of automobile archaeology, for they reflect accurately social attitudes to the motor car. In the early days they were romances, after the Great War, a harsher age appeared: in books such as Michael Arlen's *The Green Hat* and *L'Homme à l'Hispano* by Pierre Frondaie, the car—in both cases an Hispano-Suiza, most glamorous of cars—takes on an almost sentient quality, becoming a protagonist in the story rather than a simple mode of transport. Other novels of the time reflect the glamour associated with motor racing, from the authentic work of Mark Pepys, Earl of Cottenham, whose books *All Out* and *Sicilian Circuit* were based on his own racing experiences, to the penny dreadful prose of Clinton Stagg's *High Speed*, inspired by the American racing scene.

Motor rallying, too, had its literature based on actual experience; in 1932 the author John Rhode took part in the RAC Rally, in those days an event for touring vehicles and not the high speed event it has become in post war years, as part of the crew of an Armstrong Siddeley. He used the experience in his book *The Motor Rally Mystery* which covers a murder which can only be solved by applying the regulations of the rally to determine where and when the crime must have taken place.

Motoring novels still continue to have a fascination, though there is a whole world of difference between the Edwardian innocence of the *Lightning Conductor*, the hard-bitten 1920s adventures of Dornford Yates and the modern cynicism of the work of Arthur Hailey, whose novels like *Wheels* are based on close observation of the Detroit scene.

Novels of the early days can still be picked up for a few pounds, and can form an interesting specialised collection. Some of the early editions have fine illustrated covers. A collection of motoring novels covering the pre-Great War period could encompass perhaps 30 titles, although some of the early novels have become extremely rare. First editions can still be found—some of the more obscure writers failed to produce anything other than a first edition!

Unfortunately, though books such as those of the Williamsons still make entertaining reading, there is no doubt that some extremely unmechanically-minded writers were attracted to the motoring novel, padding out their lack of knowledge of the motor vehicle with improbable facts. Sometimes the result was hilarious, sometimes totally unreadable. One intriguing book which can still be found, whose author was clearly out of his depth, was the *Count's Chauffeur* by William le Queux, a prolific writer of Edwardian days whose books on spying and court intrigue could be very good but whose lack of motoring knowledge shines forth from every page. First published in serial form in 1906, the book was originally based on the exploits of a titled criminal with a Napier with an amazing variety of interchangeable bodies; it was republished in the 1920s by which time Napier were out of the motor car industry, so the name of the car was changed to Bentley without altering any of the Edwardian features of the original car! Among the other improbabilities of the car are a hero who is so resourceful that he can totally repaint his car in a matter of minutes by the roadside using a tin of enamel and a brush in order to throw a police pursuit off his track! So a collector of motoring novels must be prepared to take the dross with the gold, but will find that there is always the chance of finding some new and unexpected title.

Motoring books

It would be impossible to give a definitive list of motoring books without filling a large volume. The number of motoring books now in print runs into hundreds. Since the first motoring books, like D. Farman's 1896 *Auto-Cars*, appeared, many thousands of titles have been published. The best course for the prospective motor car book collector is to visit libraries and specialist booksellers, and to attend autojumble meets, and assess what is available, and what is of interest.

But both new and secondhand books are becoming expensive, and to build up even a modest library of two or three hundred volumes can cost several thousand pounds. Equally, catalogues, either of individual cars or of motor shows, are becoming increasingly sought after. In many cases, these are rarer that books, for they were intended as throw-away items, and were treated carelessly. Most people nowadays have to restrict themselves to 'theme' collecting, and build up a specialist library on a given marque or subject.

Some Brooklands race meeting programmes from 1922-39. On the right is an early type of programme, bearing a copy of a 1907 painting of cars at the track.

Above *Rescued from the salvage man in the early 1960s, these London motor show catalogues date from the period when the British capital had more than one annual motor exhibition. They are the 1907 Cordingley Show (held in the Agricultural Hall, Islington), the 1906 Olympia Show and the 1903 Crystal Palace Show.*

Below *Particularly rare are these Edwardian catalogues for provincial motor exhibitions in Manchester, Sheffield and Birmingham. Though the Midlands was the centre of the British car and cycle industry, the principal motor shows all took place in London— indeed, they continued to do so until 1978, when the Motor Show shifted to the new National Exhibition Centre near Birmingham.*

Early photographs

The art of photography was well established by the time the motor car arrived, consequently a considerable volume of prints of the earliest days of motoring has survived. With the growth of the auction industry, which is always seeking out new lines for auction, early photographs have gained a not entirely justified value. For the photograph is perhaps the most easily reproduced form of art that has yet been invented. Provided that one has a suitable print, even though one does not have the original negative, with modern copying equipment and fine grain film, copies can be made which are completely indistinguishable from the original. Indeed, a modern copy can in some ways appear superior as enhanced contrast can benefit an old print which has discoloured through age and make a copy appear brighter and clearer.

In the early days, large format glass plate negatives were used. These, though bulky and clumsy to use and store, had many advantages at that stage of the photographic art. For one thing, their size—some of the early motor car photographers used 10 × 8 in whole plate negatives as a matter of course—meant that any prints could be either contact prints or only a relatively small enlargement over the original negative size. This concealed the relatively coarse grain of the photographic emulsion and gave results which, for clarity, are difficult to equal today. The other advantage was that, being made from plate glass, such negatives presented an absolutely flat surface to the image, unlike roll film which can have a slight curl in it, no matter how expensive the camera.

Glass plate negatives must have been incredibly clumsy to use, and their storage poses many problems. They are, of course, extremely fragile and can crack in storage if they are stacked too high. And, to the modern collector, the type of emulsion used can pose a problem. It is possible for the emulsion to separate from the glass, in which case the negative becomes totally unusable. Equally, if the negative was not properly fixed when it was originally developed, chemical reactions will have occurred over the years which are irreversible. This can result in the negative gradually going cloudy by, in extreme cases, virtually reversing the image so that the negative becomes a positive when viewed in certain lights. The negative image can be attacked by crystals of silver nitrate efflorescing out of the emulsion. All that can be done in such cases is to have copy prints made from the negative by a skilled darkroom technician which can then be preserved or copied to give a new negative.

A skilled darkroom technician can also produce prints which are indistinguishable from 70 year old originals. By using unexpired bromide paper, 'tired' developing fluid and sepia toning the result, a print may be produced which will fool any photographic expert. Other refinements, such as aging the surface of the print by exposure to heat, should be considered by anyone tempted to pay high prices for phoney photographs at sales. Fortunately, it is still possible to acquire early photographs at reasonable prices and equally, it is still possible to come across photographs of vehicles which hitherto have remained unillustrated.

Storing old photographs can be a problem. The best way seems to be to keep them in film boxes such as sheet film is delivered in to photographic darkrooms. These boxes are strong and light proof, and will keep photographs flat until they are required. Of course, some sort of simple indexing should be followed, the easiest and most obvious of which is to store the photographs in alphabetically marked boxes. Negatives should be kept in sleeves, to protect them from dust

Showing the effects of storage in a damp cellar, this 1914 negative of a 1,094 cc Warren-Lambert light car shed its emulsion as this print was made, ending up as a blank sheet of glass.

and scratching, and glass plate negatives should be treated like vintage wine, and stored in a cool, dark, dry place, well packed in cardboard boxes.

Most early photographers worked anonymously, but some names have survived, and will be found stamped on early prints, either by a die or in ink. Campbell-Gray and Lafayette specialised in society motoring portraits, while Argent Archer of Kensington covered the whole motoring scene, from static shots of cars and components to the 1,000 Miles Trial of 1900 and the Gordon Bennett races. Between the wars, W.J. Brunell was pre-eminent—his negatives are now part of the massive photographic library at the National Motor Museum at Beaulieu.

In France, Jacques-Henri Lartigue started taking photographs as a child, and his photographs of cars and the social scene were so startlingly original in composition that they are now regarded as the work of a master artist. Two French photographic agencies achieved fame in Edwardian days—Branger, who covered all the Salons and race meetings, and Meurisse, who specialised in sporting subjects. The work of such men is wonderfully evocative: the static images they captured do much to evoke the long-dead ways of early motoring.

Moving pictures

The motor car and the moving picture arrived on the scene virtually simultaneously. With the first newsreel pictures being made around 1897, it is hardly surprising that as soon as their primitive equipment could cope with rapid movement, the pioneer film makers began to feature motor vehicles in their programmes. As early as 1903, the motor car was playing a prominent part in melodramas and comedies, and motor racing had become the subject of newsreel programmes. Early film survives from those days showing Panhards and Mercedes in events such as the Gordon Bennett Cup Races.

As technique became surer and scripts more sophisticated, increasing use was made of motor cars and they played a key role in some of the early silent comedies. The Model T Ford was especially suited to such work, as its foot operated, two-speed and reverse epicyclic gearing gave it the ability to switch from rapid forward to rapid reverse almost instantly. Also, the car was so cheap to buy on the secondhand market that it could be destroyed in a spectacular crash without setting the meagre film budget back too much. Motor racing has always been a popular subject for film makers, and much early footage survives, both of track racing and of record breaking.

Unfortunately, the stock that early film was made on is not particularly stable; generally cellulose based, it has a tendency to shrink and become brittle in storage, especially under unsuitable conditions; at its worst, the old nitrate based film can become so unstable that it will explode spontaneously when the can is opened. Even in a sound, showable condition it is still a hazard, and few cinemas are equipped nowadays to deal with it. Its high flammability obviously makes fire officers nervous, and it can invalidate the insurance of some cinemas if it is shown nowadays on equipment which is unsuited to it.

So, having discovered an old film on a motoring subject, and finding that it is worth preservation, the thing to do is to have it copied on to modern stock. This is not as easy as it seems, for there are very few processing houses nowadays who will handle nitrate based film. Equally, if it is shrunk or distorted in any way then it will have to be printed on a special machine frame by frame, and this can be exceedingly expensive. Even if one is fortunate enough to have a negative, this is not always the perfect answer, for negatives are subject to exactly the same deterioration problems as positives; and if you are having a reversal print made from a positive original, it may well be that the sound track cannot be copied because of changes in printing technique; in that case it will be necessary to have the original sound track image lifted from the film, recorded and reimposed on to the new print.

This Argent Archer photograph of the 1900 Thousand Miles' Trial shows a line-up of contestants headed by two Georges Richard cars, a Lanchester and a Panhard (RAC).

Much early film was taken on 35 mm stock; to show this, you need a specialist projector, and plenty of storage space. It is better to have old film photographically reduced to a more useful gauge, such as 16 mm (though this has a slightly different width/height ratio from 35 mm). While 8 mm films are enjoying a popularity for home movies, they are really too small for serious archive film. It is always worthwhile having old films reprinted on to modern non-inflammable stock, as their shelf life is immeasurably extended.

The motor car featured prominently in too many silent films to list individually, but it is worth noting that in 1926, a British company made a silent picture recreating the 1896 London to Brighton Run, a year before the first of the annual veteran car runs. One of the first talking pictures to have a wholly motoring theme was shot by British & Dominions Pictures in 1932, and called *The Love Contract*. Premiered at the Capitol Theatre, Haymarket, London, in August 1932, *The Love Contract* was adapted from the stage play *Chauffeur Antoinette*, and starred Winifred Shotter and Owen Nares. The plot revolved round the fact that Antoinette, played by Winifred Shotter, became chauffeur to the wealthy financier (Owen Nares) who had brought about her financial downfall. A highlight of the film was a night motor trip to Cornwall. It was noted that 'there are two very fine cars used in this film, one being a 4½-litre sports model Bentley and the other a double six Daimler fitted with a fluid flywheel and a pre-selector self-changing gearbox'. The London Morris agents, Stewart & Arden, ran a competition in conjunction with the film in which the first prize was a Morris saloon car.

Another film of the early 30s which prominently featured motor cars was *Car of Dreams*, starring Robertson Hare and John Mills. A contemporary notice of the film said: 'The car in it really is the car of many people's dreams, a beautiful *sedanca de ville* Rolls-Royce. The alleged 10,000th customer of a firm receives the car for nothing, and sundry other complications followed, including Robertson Hare as a trombone tester. It ends with an awe-inspiring trip down a bypass, followed by a trip—still in the Rolls-Royce—amongst the clouds'.

In 1979, the world's first motor film archive was set up by the National Motor Museum at Beaulieu: its contents include the Ford film archive (approximately 1,000 reels of 35 mm positive and negative film covering the period 1930-70) and films from Castrol and other film libraries. One 'horror film' I was shown by the Museum's film archivist was a 1920s nitrate three-reeler rescued after a fire at the Austin factory at Longbridge. Preserved by a fireproof box, it had charred like the outer wrappings of a mummy.

Music

To celebrate the production of the ten millionth Model T Ford in 1924, composer F.S. Converse decided, for his own amusement, to produce a symphony which he entitled *Flivver Ten Million*. Converse described the work as a 'joyous epic fantasy for orchestra'. It was first performed by the Boston Symphony Orchestra early in 1927, when a music critic referred to some of the passages as being of great musical beauty though 'it is possible that the piece might have a musical appeal if the "story" (and the motor horn) were deleted! On a more frivolous note, a former violinist named De Groot adopted the stage name 'Stenelli' and appeared on the music halls in the 1930s with his 'Hornchestra', playing melodies on tuned bulb and electric motor horns . . ..

Motoring was a popular theme with composers of light music. Jack Glogan, 'composer of King Sol, etc', wrote a motoring march called *The Pace that Kills*, published in Chicago in the early 1900s, while one Claude Terrasse composed a Teuf-Teuf-Marche entitled *Cent-Vingt a l'Heure*. In Italy, L.A. Villanis wrote *L'Automobile*, with words by Frâ Kanapa. 'One make' compositions included *The Ford March and Two-Step*, written around 1908 and a 1930s advertising song *Rhythm of the Road*, composed for King Palmer's V8 Shadow Symphony orchestra—the first orchestra named for a car model—which played at the Ford Motor Show in London's Albert Hall in 1936.

Gramophone records

Though the motor car might seem to be an unusual subject for gramophone recordings, it was the subject of a number of music hall turns in the early days, some of which found their way on to record; I remember many years ago that our family had one of those curious Durium cardboard records, single-sided with a plastic track on it which featured a music hall song called *Sweatin' on my old Selinda*, apparently based on the misfortunes of a singer with his De Dion Bouton car. I remember the refrain of this song went something like 'Ha ha ha, He he he, Little brown plug. How I love thee'. Another early record to feature motoring was a so-called comedy monologue called *Winkelheimer's Motor Ride* by Tom Clare, which seems to reflect fairly vividly the fears of the early motorist. In similar vein was *Cohen is arrested for exceeding the speed limit* by Joe Hayman, on Regal. *Motoring without tears* was a duologue between L. Dugarde Peach and Hermione Baddeley. This is gentle satire on the motoring manners of the 1920s, and it is an oral account of a somewhat trouble-fraught driving lesson on 'a sweet little car'.

Cars featured on dance records, too, with titles such as *The Love Song of the Packard and the Ford, I'm wild about horns that go da-di-di-da,* and *Henry's Made a Lady out of Lizzie* (to mark the replacement of the Model T Ford by the modern Model A in 1928). Perhaps the rarest motoring record of all is the 1926 recording of the Gus Edwards hit song *In My Merry Oldsmobile*. This was recorded by Jean Goldkette and his orchestra, to publicise the new Oldsmobile range, and a copy of the record was intended to be given away with each new car. However, this proved to be a somewhat misguided publicity stunt, as the fragile 78 records often arrived broken at their destinations and were considered too much of a nuisance by the dealers, who failed to put them in the cars in the majority of cases; those very few owners who did take delivery of the car complete with the record usually managed to sit on the disc on the journey home from the showrooms, so that this particular recording achieved almost legendary status both on account of its rarity and because the cornettist with the band on this occasion was the celebrated Bix Beiderbecke. In fact, the world stock of this particular recording seems to have all emanated from the same source; an unsold 1926 Oldsmobile which languished for many years in a dealership gathering dust, with half-a-dozen of the precious records in its glove compartment. It has since been reissued on an LP by RCA.

Motoring art

Though Leonardo sketched designs for clockwork carriages, probably the first illustration of an actual self-propelled vehicle was an engraving of Hans Hautsch's Triumphwagen built in Nuremburg in 1649. Seemingly driven by a system of gearing operated by men concealed within the bodywork (though

One of the earliest illustrations of a self-propelled vehicle, Johann Hautsch's Nuremberg Triumphwagen of the 17th century.

some reports attributed its motive force to clockwork) the Triumphwagen could cover 2,000 paces in an hour. The engraving shows it to have been a complicated and cumbersome vehicle with its forward part carved into the shape of a sea monster.

The first great outpouring of automotive art coincided with the Golden Age of Steam in the 1820s and 1830s. A number of hand coloured lithographs and etchings appeared depicting steam carriages drawn with a fair degree of artistic licence. Among the known artists were J. Doyle, who drew Gurney's *New Steam Carriage as it appeared at Hounslow on the 12 August with a Barouche attached containing the Duke of Wellington and other persons of distinction,* I.D. Jones, who drew a pair of illustrations entitled *The London Steam Carriage* and *The Edinburgh Steam Carriage,* G. Morton, W. Summers and John Cook (who drew a highly fanciful rendering of *Dr Church's London— Birmingham Steam Coach* which almost certainly never ran, and certainly was never finished). Even the celebrated satirist George Cruikshank caricatured the steam carriage craze in an etching entitled *The Horses "Going to the Dogs".*

Coloured lithographs enjoyed a renaissance in the early motor age, popularised by the French artist, Ernest Montaut and his protégé, Gamy. The work of these two artists covered many subjects. Montaut (who died aged only

30, in 1909) specialised in racing scenes, covering events like the Gordon Bennett, Paris-Madrid, the Vanderbilt Cup, the Targa Florio, the Coupe des Voiturettes, the Grand Prix and Brooklands racing. Though his drawings were not always accurate, they displayed tremendous life and vigour. Montaut was the first motoring artist, apparently, to capture movement by deliberate distortion of the car's image. His best work appeared in a little book called *10 Ans de Course*, but he also issued many larger hand-coloured lithographs. Several of the more outstanding lithographs were reissued recently in reproduction form. Gamy seems to have concentrated more on touring subjects than Montaut, and was possibly the better artist of the two. Both men were backed by a studio of some size, essential to the mass production of illustrations, reportedly by the 'pochoir' process in which only the outline of the drawing was printed by lithography, the colours being added by hand by workers using a series of specially cut stencils.

Motoring lithographs of a more conventional type were produced especially in France where artists such as Albert Robida, Henri-Georges Meunier and André Nevil created illustrations inspired by motoring incidents. Meunier's 1905 lithograph *Bloqués*, for instance, depicts a motorist impeded by a herd of sheep. British artists working in this genre included Cecil Aldin, better known for his hunting and dog illustrations and Harry Elliot, who produced some very atmospheric, if slightly naive, illustrations of early motor racing subjects.

The work of Montaut and Gamy was often used by manufacturers to publicise

Only loosely based on contemporary fact, Alken's Illustration of Modern Prophecy— The Progress of steam *was an 1830 vision of future traffic in London's Whitechapel Road.*

Left *Painted in the late 1890s, this illustration by Robida shows the joys of automobilism on a sunny day. A companion painting showed the reverse side of the coin—motoring in a downpour!*

Right *The artist, Jean Routier, noted for his humorous sketches of motoring subjects, illustrated this 1920 advertisement for the prestigious French motoring magazine* Automobilia.

their products; so too were drawings by René Vincent, perhaps the most gifted of all the commercial artists of motoring. Vincent, who was born in 1879, was employed by manufacturers such as Peugeot, Ford, Berliet and Delahaye to produce advertising and catalogue illustrations. His inimitable drawings captured the manners of the age and Berliet used several series of his drawings in the form of lithographs, presumably primarily for display in their agencies. Such series showed Berliet cars in use all round the world, ridden in by caricatured inhabitants of various countries.

One of Vincent's most popular illustrations was a pair of lithographs issued in 1915 entitled *Le Départ de l'Ambusque* and *Le Rétour de l'Ambusque* which depicted two young men setting off in their immaculate Peugeot car to war and returning in the same car considerably battered with a huge pile of German guns and helmets with honourably-won bandages. He also created some memorable Peugeot advertisements.

The other great French commercial artist was Geo Ham (Georges Hamel), Vincent's junior by 21 years. His work is best known in the form of posters and catalogue illustrations, but he was also capable of turning out elegant watercolour studies of cars, as well as caricatures of racing drivers. Roughly contemporary with Ham but slightly 'harder' in style was the Russian-born artist and car stylist, Alexis Kow, who began his career as a publicity artist in Paris in 1922, with Panhard, Pirelli and DFP as his first clients. He was,

Early motor racing scenes depicted by Harry Elliott. Though perhaps a little stilted, his work still manages to capture the drama of racing on the open highway.

apparently, still designing publicity material for Paris-Rhône, the electrical component manufacturers, 50 years later.

There were British artists active in the period 1910-30 who are worth noting: Guy Lipscomb, for example, best known for his magazine illustrations, also produced some spirited paintings of motor cars. Lipscomb, who later became a Royal Academician of note, also drew what is generally regarded as the first cutaway drawing of an automobile component—a Longuemare carburettor, published in *The Motor* in 1909.

Around 1910 pen and ink drawings signed by John Bryan began appearing in *The Motor*. Bryan subsequently changed his name to Bryan de Grineau and contributed under that name to *The Motor* in the 1920s, 30s and 40s. De Grineau was a very rapid worker and could turn out an editorial illustration in a very short space of time. *The Motor* was particularly advanced in the 1920s in using an aeroplane to fly copy (and de Grineau) back to London from Continental race meetings. De Grineau could apparently produce a detailed sketch of a racing incident in an hour or so, aboard the wallowing Sopwith or De Havilland, ready for publication when the plane touched down. Unfortunately, much of de Grineau's work was apparently destroyed during office moves at Temple Press, publishers of *The Motor*. Oddly enough, the change of name from John Bryan resulted in a change of style; most of the 'John Bryan' work was executed in pen and ink, while the Bryan de Grineau drawings were in charcoal and wash or pencil.

In the 1920s and 1930s, the two great rivals were *The Motor* and *The Autocar*; and *The Autocar* boasted a better artist than de Grineau in Frederick Gordon

Left *This 1926 Salmson advertisement features drawings by Alexis Kow, who subsequently turned his hand to car styling (as did C.F. Beauvais, who worked for* The Motor *before turning stylist in the early 1930s).*

Below *The art of the cutaway drawing has progressed greatly since Guy Lipscombe made the first cutaway (a drawing of a carburettor) in 1909. This drawing of the 1934 Grand Prix Alfa Romeo was made by the French artist Gedovius, known as 'G. Gedo'.*

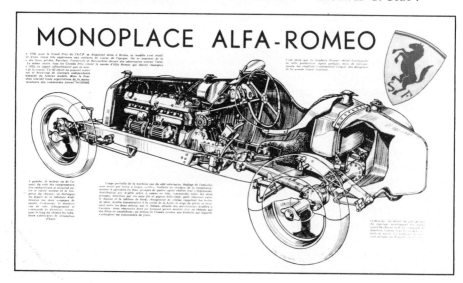

MONOPLACE ALFA-ROMEO

Crosby, who again had had his first work published in the paper before the Great War. Crosby—known as 'Gorby' to his friends—could draw cars better than any artist before or since, imparting a sense of action into his paintings which no-one else has been able to imitate. He was an artist of wide-ranging skills: his work for *The Autocar* included front cover advertisements, cut-away drawings of chassis; pen and ink drawings and perhaps his greatest achievement, his full colour plates which were given away with the magazine in two series—*Meteors of Road and Track* and *The Endless Quest for Speed*. Crosby also designed the radiator badge for the Bentley car and the original leaping Jaguar mascot, as well as turning out a number of bronze sculptures and bas-reliefs. In 1932 *The Autocar* noted: '*The Daily Telegraph* has presented to the BARC a challenge trophy designed by Mr. F. Gordon Crosby, of *The Autocar*, to be given to the driver who holds the record for the highest speed for one lap of the Brooklands "mountain" course. Unlike most trophies, this one is thoroughly suitable for its object. It is probably the finest piece of work Mr. Crosby has produced, and it shows the modern type racing car in violent action on a corner better than bronze has ever shown this before, without undue or noticeable exaggeration being indulged in, but with an effect that is almost startling.

'It is fitting that Sir Henry Birkin, Bt should be the first holder, for among British drivers no man has a better record of laps at high speed, and that record extends over many different classes of race. His present record on the "mountain" circuit was made with the Maserati on August 3 last year at a rate of 75.21 mph, which is one lap in 56 seconds, and a speed almost incredible to those who remember the start of "mountain" racing, even allowing for the fact that the 2,765 cc Maserati is an eminently suitable machine for this record.' In 1979, this trophy was sold at Christies for £2,500. A definitive biography of Crosby was published in 1978 by Hamlyns (*The Art of Gordon Crosby* by Peter Garnier).

America has produced some noted motoring artists too: the work of Carlo Demand has been widely published, while in earlier days that noted commercial artist, Edward Penfield, produced some fine artwork for Pierce Arrow. But unquestionably the outstanding American artist in the automotive field is Peter Helck, still active at the time of writing, in his 80s. Helck's first illustrations were executed while he was still a boy, around 1906 and, like Gordon Crosby, he is obviously happiest dealing with 'the heroic age' of motoring. Helck learnt his art in America and in England, where he studied under Sir Frank Brangwyn, whose influence can be seen in Helck's bold use of colour. Helck is certainly a better draughtsman than Crosby in many respects, especially in his figure work, though his paintings tend to be less 'free' in style and his cars do not have the same violent sense of movement as those in Crosby's work.

Other excellent artists included H.J. Moser, whose vivid covers made the short-lived 1930s magazine *Speed* so attractive (*Speed*, founded in June 1935, was absorbed into *Motor Sport*, which had been founded in 1924 as *The Brooklands Gazette*), Roy Nockolds and Terence Cuneo. Count Carlo Biscaretti di Ruffia, founder of the Turin Museum, was also a skilled artist: in the latter years of his life he recreated historic incidents in charming watercolours. One of the few modern artists whose work can be compared w' the masters like Crosby and De Grineau is Michael Wright, whose schoolboy efforts appeared in *Speed* in the mid-1930s. Unashamedly h' in subject, his paintings have a distinct style while dramatically evoking bygone glories. Motoring art is definitely on the move: 20 years ago it was admired by only a dedicated few. Today, Crosby originals can fetch four-figure sums.

Posters

The first motor car posters seem to have advertised events rather than vehicles. The 1896 exhibition in London's Imperial Institute, for example, was promoted by a poster carrying a goddess of speed in an unstable two-wheeled winged chariot similar to that depicted on the medal awarded by H.J. Lawson to competitors in the London to Brighton run held later that year, and also shown on the licensing plates issued by his Motoring Manufacturing Company. As a piece of art it was fairly dreadful, but later motor meets, such as the 1897 Automobile Club Show in Richmond's Old Deer Park had neater art work in the Dudley Hardy idiom.

It was on the continent, however, that really distinguished poster artists began to give their attention to motoring subjects. Jules Chéret, for instance, produced a poster for a fuel called 'Benzo-Motor' around 1900, depicting a girl— one of his celebrated 'Chérettes'—at the wheel of a motor car being overtaken by a Piéper voiturette, while the Belgian Privat-Livemont designed a highly stylised *art nouveau* automobiliste to promote the Paris Salon de l'Automobile in 1902.

The first great flowering of the motor car poster was in France in the first decade of the century. Manufacturers such as Hurtu, Gladiator, Clement and Richard Brasier all issued striking publicity posters by the leading artists of the day. In the late 1890s, De Dion Bouton issued a series of posters showing their vehicles in various unlikely situations, which acquired a certain notoriety for the subjects depicted, such as a mother suckling her baby while travelling along in a De Dion Bouton voiturette. Abel Faivre, a celebrated artist in pastels, created a charming poster for the 1905 Paris Salon, with a girl in an ermine cape being driven in a voiturette by a youthful chauffeur clad in a *'peau de bique'* (a goatskin coat with the fur side outside).

In the 1920s and 1930s, posters in general became more 'commercial', though the work of Ham and Vincent was consistently good, and artists like René Révo, A.E. Marty and Gérold produced excellent work, too. The Shell Oil Company's posters of the 1930s were of a high standard too, employing leading artist of the day on both motoring and landscape subjects. Some of the more famous were reissued by Shell in the 1960s.

Above right *An early (1907) poster for the celebrated Spanish made, Hispano-Suiza. The Hispano achieved its greatest renown in the 1920s when it was also produced at Bois-Colombes, Paris. Designer, Marc Birkigt, was Swiss, hence the name.*

Above far right *Oswald Cuningham painted a number of these light-hearted posters for Ford (England) circa 1915 on the theme 'Sell it and buy a Ford'. At that time the Model T Ford was Britain's best-selling car, with over 6,000 produced in 1913 at the Trafford Park, Manchester, factory.*

Right *This early De Dion Bouton poster advertises Count Mortimer Megret's De Dion Manual, with which 'the De Dion Bouton car goes everywhere without breaking down'. Mortimer Megret also compiled one of the first lists dating early cars, for the Anglo-French* Automobilia *magazine in 1906.*

SOCIÉTE PARISIENNE
CYCLES
VOITURETTES
10, AUE DE LA GDE ARMEE
PARIS

By Motor Car, By Aeroplane, By Motor Boat
STANDARD PETROL & MOVRIL
WILL SPEED YOU WELL.

"THE SPIRIT OF THE TIME SHALL TEACH ME SPEED." King John, Act IV, Scene II.

LUBRICATING OILS AND GREASES,
CARLESS CAPEL & LEONARD,
HACKNEY WICK, LONDON, N.E.

Telephone 1310 EAST.

A16   MENTION OF "THE AUTOCAR," WHEN WRITING TO ADVERTISERS, WILL ENSURE PROMPT ATTENTION.

Left *Despite the carefree atmosphere of this turn-of-the-century poster, the 'Victoria Combination', built by the Société Parisienne, was a particularly beastly device, which used the engine and rear axle of a De Dion tricycle as a front-wheel-drive 'power pack'. As this entire unit pivoted when the tiller was operated, the Victoria Combination (sold in Britain as the 'Eureka Voiturette') was highly unstable.* **Above** *A 1910 poster issued by Carless, Capel & Leonard of London, who first coined the word 'petrol' to describe motor spirit.* **Below** *The Unic name is still seen on trucks today, but it first appeared in 1905 when the engineer, Georges Richard, launched a new model, having just broken away from the Richard-Brasier concern. Only one type of chassis was manufactured, hence the name—'unique'.*

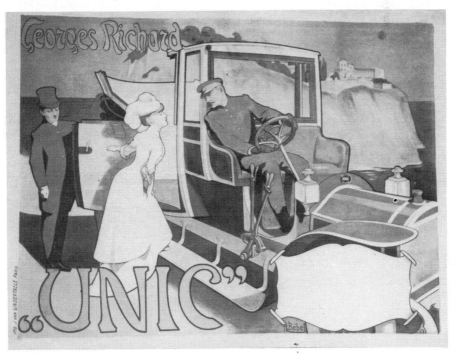

Postcards

A more modest form of motoring art is the picture postcard, which appeared at the same time as the motor car, and featured many early motoring subjects. Especially sought-after are the sets depicting early motor races. The heyday of the picture postcard was the period up to the end of the Great War, but in recent years some of the early advertising postcards have been reissued by French companies. In 1980, an English company issued a 1932 Ford advertisement 'The Greatest Thrill in Motoring' as a postcard.

Sculptures

When newspaper tycoon James Gordon Bennett (he was the proprietor of the *New York Herald*, and had sent Stanley to find Livingstone) inaugurated an international motor racing contest in 1900, he commissioned the silversmith Aucoc to produce a magnificent trophy in the shape of a racing Panhard careering along in a cloud of dust with a goddess of speed standing on the seat. The trophy, a massive silver casting, was impressively accurate. Made by the lost wax process, it was complete down to riveted-on steps, drop arm and drag link for the steering, bulb horn and pedal. Even the gear change quadrant was correctly notched.

Each one of the winners driving during the five years that the Gordon Bennett Cup Series was held received a bronze replica of this statue; the only British driver to win the Gordon Bennett was S.F. Edge, the bombastic Australian-born motor trader who masterminded the sales of Napiers. He won in 1902, mainly because there was so little interest in the race that year. His copy of the Gordon Bennett trophy stood for many years on the staircase of his London office; after his death, it was presented to the Veteran Car Club by his widow. It is now a prized exhibit in their headquarters at Ashwell, Hertfordshire. The 'genuine' Gordon Bennett Trophy resides in Paris, in the palatial premises of the Automobile Club de France.

The Gordon Bennett Trophy and the equally elaborate Coppa della Velocita sculpted for Vincenzo Florio by Polak in 1905 are among the most spectacular examples of early motoring sculpture to have survived. However, in the early years of the century, racing cars were a popular subject for sculptors in the shape of attractive desk tidies, concealing ink wells beneath their bonnets. Typical examples were a De Diétrich, whose driver carried the cross of Lorraine on his chest, so that it looked like the frogging on a military greatcoat, and a magnificently modelled Mercedes, by W. Zwick, in the Art Nouveau idiom, and produced in a limited edition, with either silver or bronze finish. These two models were perhaps the most outstanding although there were other models of small touring cars of the De Dion type, some of them fairly crudely modelled, and including an odd ink well which reproduced only the bonnet, seat and driver of a motor car, being totally devoid of wheels or chassis, and really not having a great deal of artistic merit.

There were also motoring mantlepiece ornaments, in the idiom of the day; apparently produced in at least two series, these featured an Art Nouveau goddess standing precariously on the dashboard of a two-wheeled motor car and were part of a set of four allegorical models depicting *'L'Automobile,'* *'L'Aviation'*, *'Le Rail'* and *'Le Bateau.'* The smaller models were much cruder in execution than the larger, though the subjects were similar. *'L'Aviation'* shows a scantily-clad Greek god standing on the fuselage of a somewhat skimpy

Bleriot monoplane, while *'L'Automobile'* represents an Art Nouveau goddess perched precariously on the dashboard of a two-wheeled motor car careering along without visible means of support.

Another motoring sculpture of the early days of considerable merit was the Henry Edmunds Trophy, which depicts a racing Renault of Paris-Vienna type, and appears to have been the work of the same sculptor as the Mercedes mentioned above. The Henry Edmunds trophy was presented to the Automobile Club of Great Britain and Ireland (later the RAC) in 1902 by Henry Edmunds, who was then a member of the club committee, for contest at hillclimb events. The trophy was awarded as follows: July 7 1903, Castlewellan, Ireland—E. Campbell Muir (Mercedes); 1904, no competition; September 27 1905, Blackdown House, C. Grinham (Daimler); July 14 1906, Blackdown House, G.S. Barwick (Daimler); July 8 1907, Underriver, Sevenoaks, G.S. Barwick (Daimler); 1908, no competition; July 17 1909, Shelsley Walsh, A.J. Hancock (Vauxhall); July 2 1910, Shelsley Walsh, R. Lyle (Star); 1911, 1912 and 1913, no competition; June 10 and 11 1914, Isle of Man, K. Lee Guinness, (Sunbeam). In the 1914 competition, the Henry Edmunds trophy was offered as a prize in the Isle of Man Tourist Trophy race, and was won by Ken Lee Guinness on the racing Sunbeam by reason of his making the best aggregate time during the sixteen laps of the 16 ascents of the hill between Ramsey and the bungalow on Snae Fell.

In 1905, in collaboration with *La Vie au Grand Air*, the *Dépêche de Toulouse* organised a touring event for cars under the name 'Coupe de Pyrénées.' Each competitor was given a souvenir which was 'original and particularly artistic' in the shape of a medallion with, on one side, an illustration of a car touring in the Pyrénées and, on the other side, an allegorical figure representing the activities of the newspaper *La Dépêche*. The designer of the medallion was Louis Oury, an artist from Montauban. The principal trophy for the event, the Coupe des Pyrénées, was designed by the sculptor Ducuing, and fashioned in silver by Barbédienne. Measuring 90 × 65 centimetres the statue weighed 35 kilograms. It depicted Pyrène, the legendary fairy who was the lover of Hercules, who was supposed to have thrown up the Pyrénées. Clad in no more than an artistically flowing ribbon, Pyrène was seated in a curious 'classical' motor car in the shape of a shell with four wheels, upholstered with a polar bear skin and whose only concession to modernity was a steering wheel. The trophy was won by one M. Sorel, who had previously won a race from Delhi to Bombay at the wheel of his 40 hp De Diétrich.

Another elegant trophy of the same year was the Coupe de Compiègne, presented by the Automobile Club de l'Oise for the first vehicle in the general class of the Concours de Tourisme. It depicted a motorist on a dais, with a miniature motor car behind him, being crowned with a laurel wreath by a classical goddess. Winner of this trophy was Baron Petiet, driving an Aries.

Also found at this period were flat trays with bas-relief sculptures of racing cars and plaques of similar style which were often given as prizes in motoring competitions. A particularly fine example of the plaque is the Prince Henry trophy, awarded by Prince Henry of Prussia for the touring car contest bearing his name, a splendid piece of silver work which was won in 1909 by Ettore Bugatti driving a Hermes-Simplex of his own design shortly before he set up as a manufacturer on his own account. Another plaque of the early days showed a racing car with a speed goddess in the sky overhead; this was awarded to Charles

Jarrott for his epic drive from London to Monte Carlo in 37½ hours in a 40 hp Crossley car in April 1906; his record was broken the next month by the Honourable C.S. Rolls on a Rolls TT car who cut two minutes (!) off Jarrott's time. However, many years later, Jarrott's mechanic, H.P. Small, remarked to me that Rolls had only broken Jarrott's record because he failed to observe the speed limits. Incidentally, in June 1906, H.R. Pope, on an Itala, cut the record to 36 hours 5 minutes. Jarrott took it back again in 1907, in 35 hours 5 minutes, in a Crossley, only to lose it first to M. Auriac (Napier) in 33 hours 34 minutes, then to H.R. Pope (Itala) who cut the time to an astonishing 29 hours 16 minutes. Replicas of this plaque were produced in France in the 1960s.

An unusual form of motoring art was reported by *The Car Illustrated* in 1908. The magazine complained that: 'In their delineation of automobiles, very few artists have so far succeeded in conveying that sense of speed and power which appeals so strongly to the observer when actually watching the progress of a car. Even racing subjects have been poorly handled as a rule.' However, the magazine had just been shown some repoussé work in silver carried out by 'a clever London artist', Frank Lutiger. Lutiger was reported to have produced 'some wonderfully striking picture of automobile subjects', and his work was illustrated in the magazine by a silver panel depicting a De Diétrich racing car at speed. The magazine noticed that the detail work was marvellously accurate. Finished in dull silver, Lutiger's plaque was very much in the idiom of the contemporary Montaut prints.

Other media than metal were used by sculptors to depict the motor car; the French artist P. Moreau-Vauthier produced a fine ceramic model of Gabriel's Paris-Madrid Mors racer, in blue-green salt glaze pottery (which was produced by the ceramist Emile Decoeur), while in 1907 Moreau-Vauthier sculpted a remarkably accurate model of Thery's Gordon Bennett winning Richard Brasier car in terra cotta, a material then much in vogue for facing motor car factories. However, the accuracy of rendition of the car was somewhat nullified by the allegorical female figures rising out of the dust cloud in its wake with clutching hands.

Although motoring sculpture did survive the Great War, it went into a decline and the last pieces of any consequence were produced in the mid-1930s. However, some fine sculptures do survive from the 1920s, notably a splendid representation of a racing Sunbeam car by the Belgian artist, P. de Soëte, dating from 1922. Accurately modelled, and full of life and movement, this statue is on a par with any of the pre-war examples. There also survive some delicate table top models of Renault cars, little bronzes apparently made as presents for VIP customers of the Renault works.

A sculpture with a history was presented to Oxford MP, Frank Gray, in 1927. Mr Gray and J. Sawyer had just completed a 3,500-mile crossing of Africa in two Jowett cars named *'Wait'* and *'See'*. During the course of his journey they liberated an African girl from slave traders, and Sir George Beharrell of the Dunlop Rubber Company presented a casket to Gray to commemorate his successful crossing from Lagos, Nigeria, to Massawa on the Red Sea in 58 days, 'suffering many hardships in the long journey over swamp and desert'. The presentation was in the form of a casket hand-worked in silver with bronze slaves in chains at the corners and a model of the Jowett car on the top.

A novel award was given to winners of the Motor Cycle Club's 'Triple Award', for motor cyclists or motorists who had won Gold Medals in the

London-Exeter, London-Lands End and London-Edinburgh trials. The award consisted of a silver relief map of Great Britain mounted on an ebony plaque, with the routes of the three classic trials traced in red enamel. Ten inches long, the plaque was designed by Bertie Marians, the famous trials motor cyclist, and was first awarded in 1927. However, the award was quite optional, and the winners could still have their three gold medals if they preferred. Incidentally, Bertie Marians was driving the 1910 Model T Ford now owned by the Ford Motor Company in front of the Dublin Post Office in 1916 when its windscreen was shot away by a sniper's bullet—and that is why the car has, to this day, the wrong pattern of windscreen fitted.

Perhaps the last motoring sculptures of any merit were created by F. Gordon Crosby and were apparently given as trophies by *The Autocar* for whom Crosby worked. Crosby's sculptures are almost caricatures, yet display that love of accuracy which is evident in his drawn work; indeed it is on record that Crosby destroyed one of his models before it could be cast in bronze because the ever alert sports editor of *The Autocar*, Sammy Davis, had pointed out to him that the drag link was in the wrong position relative to the angle of the front wheels of the car! Gordon Crosby also designed a memorial plaque for Sir Henry Birkin, which the British Racing Drivers' Club placed on the wall of the club house at Brooklands. The memorial was unveiled in June 1934, by Lord Howe.

Trophies for the more successful driver represented something of a nuisance, occupying much space and requiring frequent cleaning. The late E.C. Gordon England had a neat solution to the problem. When he retired from racing in the 1920s, he had all his silver trophies melted down and refashioned by a craftsman silversmith into an *art déco* dinner service, each knife, fork or spoon having engraved on it the name of the race for which the trophy it had been made from had been awarded.

Lord Perry's Punchbowl

Late in 1979, a remarkable silver punchbowl and stand appeared at Ford's European headquarters in Warley, Essex. The property of the Perry family, it had been presented to Lord Perry, Chairman of Ford of Britain, in 1938 as a unique record of the '1928 Plan' which set up Ford's first European organisation. It bore the engraved signatures of directors and managers of the national companies controlled from the office of Sir Percival Perry in Regent Street, London, these being represented by their national flags. In a particularly unfortunate piece of juxtaposition (at least by modern standards), the Union Jack overlay the German Swastika . . . .

Apart from Henry and Edsel Ford, there are the signatures of some distinguished men on the tray: Lord Illingworth (Director of the National Provincial Bank), Sir Roland Kitson (Director of the Bank of England), Sir John T. Davies (Director of the Suez Canal Company), Maurice Dollfuss (banker and director of Hispano-Suiza), Jean Charles Carpentier (director of Credit Mobilier Francais), Dr Carl Bosch (General Manager of IG Farben) and August Philips (the leading Dutch industrialist) were among the outside Directors serving on national Ford company boards. Camille Gutt, on the Belgian board, would later become head of the International Monetary Fund; Heinrich Albert, 'founding father' of Ford Germany, had been a Cabinet Minister during the Weimar Republic. The Ford employees who signed the tray have become legendary names in Company history; 'Cast Iron' Charlie

This elaborate silver-plated punchbowl, presented to Ford-Britain Chairman, Lord Perry, in 1938, bears the engraved signatures of Henry and Edsel Ford, as well as the signatures of the executives of the European Ford companies controlled by Perry's London office.

Sorensen, for 40 years one of Henry Ford's closest associates, Patrick Hennessy, Rowland Smith and Stanford Cooper, all to become Chairman of Ford of Britain after Perry.

Personal effects

For many years it has been the practice for manufacturers and organisers of sporting events to issue miniature badges to be worn in the lapel buttonhole; these served various purposes, such as advertising a particular marque, identifying its salesmen at motor shows, acting as a souvenir of a sporting event, or identifying fully paid-up members of a motoring organisation. The latter was the reason why the Brooklands Automobile Racing Club issued its members annually with lapel badges whose design changed from year to year. The first BARC badges appeared in 1907, the year the track was opened, and consisted of a black lozenge with yellow lettering; in the last year of the track's activity, 1939, the badge showed a head-on view of a racing car. Competitors in pre-war RAC rallies were issued with enamelled badges, usually in the RAC colours of blue and white, and differing in design according to the year; one year a pennant shape was used, another year the legend 'RAC Rally' appeared on a rectangle.

The event which really established motor touring in America was the Glidden Tour, and the lapel badge for this event showed the Glidden Trophy, awarded by Charles J. Glidden, depicting the globe, supported by a caryatid, topped by the Napier car in which he set out to girdle the world in 1902, covering 46,000 miles in two seasons. Handsomely cast from bronze, and finely detailed, the Glidden Trophy was perhaps one of the most attractive ever issued.

Lapel badges in the form of miniature radiator badges were issued at some time or another by virtually every make of car; in recent years, French enthusiasts have reissued a number of early radiator badges for marque enthusiasts. Badges also depicted chauffeurs' heads, M Bibendum, the Michelin man, and various makes of car. In 1908 the London accessory company, S. Smith & Son, advertised a brooch in the shape of a Daimler car covered in brilliants. A tie sticker exists in the shape of a racing car with 'Dieppe' inscribed on it, which would have been a souvenir of the 1908 Grand Prix, while the 'Red Devil' Camille Jenatzy commemorated his win in the 1903 Gordon Bennett Race by producing not only a small medal of the sort hung on watch chains depicting his victorious Mercedes (and advertising Jenatzy tyres at the same time) but also offered a penknife depicting the car.

Buttons cast from brass and depicting various unidentifiable early motor cars were produced for chauffeurs' uniforms. Other accessories for the well-turned-out motorist included letter seals in the shape of Mercedes or Panhard radiators, a goggled automobilist at the wheel of his car. To celebrate the construction of their 25,000th single-cylinder engine in 1901, De Dion Bouton produced small cast models of the engine suitable for use as paper weights. These well-detailed models have now become scarce, though for many years one was visible in the window of a tyre shop in North Croydon, Surrey. It vanished when the shop was closed down in the early 1960s. During the 1920s, R.W. Coan, of Islington, who pioneered aluminium castings in Britain, used to give Christmas presents in the form of little trays cast of aluminium; because of his close connection with the motor trade, some of these depicted motoring subjects, including the

Below left *This lapel badge is an exact miniature of the Glidden Trophy and depicts Charles J. Glidden's Napier car encircling the world* (Foulkes-Halbard Collection).

Below right *This elaborate badge was worn by the assistant secretary of the 1901 Liverpool Trials of the Self-Propelled Traffic Association which pioneered the introduction of motor goods vehicles in the north-west of England.*

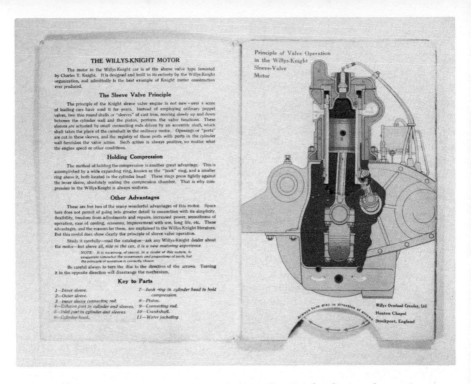

Above *This working cardboard model of the Willys-Knight sleeve valve engine was a 1920s 'giveaway' to explain the sleeve-valve principle to prospective customers.* **Below** *'The modern stirrup-cup'—a French plate dating from circa 1913* (Foulkes-Halbard Collection). **Above right** *This silver match-case and brooch, made in Birmingham in 1901, probably depict an actual car, and were doubtless commissioned by the owner to depict his latest automobile. Note the authentic detailing, such as the brake rod passing through the rear mudguard, which could not have been invented by a silversmith working in the abstract* (Foulkes-Halbard Collection). **Right** *A souvenir dashboard plaque awarded to Malcolm Campbell for his participation in the 1923 speed trials on Fano Island, off Denmark* (Foulkes-Halbard Collection). **Below right** *A china egg by Meissen with a motoring illustration based on a cartoon by the British artist, Will Owen* (Foulkes-Halbard Collection).

Brooklands records set up in 1922 by J.A. Joyce driving an AC single-seater.

Valentin, *'Roi des Caoutchoucs'* ('the rubber King'), who apparently offered some form of waterproof clothing, presented his customers with an elaborate ashtray depicting himself riding in his *Coupé Carrosse* Voisin, one of those typical follies of the 1920s in which the rear part of the chauffeur driven car resembled a 17th century stage coach, hung on leather cee-springs. A moulded brass ashtray was issued circa 1920 depicting a touring car at speed between trees. An unfortunate practice consisted of turning out the threads from inside brass hubcaps and filing cigarette rests on the lip to create an ashtray.

Watches depicting motor cars were fairly common in the early days of motoring. In 1896 a Swiss company offered an elaborately decorated watch with a picture of a motor car—a Benz double phaeton equipped with a canopy—while two years later a French company announced the Automobile Watch, 'for punctual chauffeurs', which carried a representation of a motor car on its face.

Ornamented cases became popular in the early years of the century. Around 1904 a French company offered a watch with a face whose lid depicted the victorious Richard Brasier driven by Thery in the Gordon Bennett Cup, 1909, a similar type of watch depicted a touring Rochet Schneider at speed. From Swiss makers came another Rochet Schneider of slightly earlier date, a double phaeton of around 1904-5 shown at speed on a country road. Similar in concept was the 1907 Swiss watch whose case depicted a four-seater NAG phaeton.

The exhibitor's pass used by Gottlieb Daimler at the 1893 Columbian Exposition in Chicago. The German inventor was attempting to establish an American market for his cars, and in fact some engine assembly was undertaken by the Steinway Piano Company in New York in the 1890s.

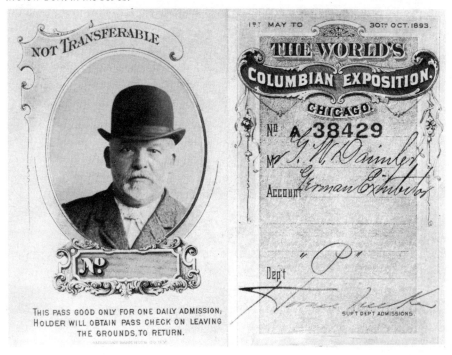

Above left *A timekeeper's watch from the 1903 Gordon Bennett Race held in Ireland in 1903 and won by 'Red Devil' Camille Jenatzy on a 60 hp Mercedes borrowed after a works fire had destroyed his 90 hp racer* (Foulkes-Halbard Collection).

Above right *This Peugeot ashtray of the 1920s incorporates a humorous mascot based on the company's lion symbol* (Foulkes-Halbard Collection).

Clocks with motor car features are rare; however, the Ariel-Simplex Company produced advertising clocks in the first decade of this century in which the figures on the face of the clock were replaced by the letters Ariel-Simplex, and an illustration of the car was lithographed on to the face of the clock.

Another curious time-piece (or rather distance measure) was the Live-Map-Meter produced around 1910 by the makers of Jones speedometers. Eight inches in diameter, the Live-Map-Meter resembled a giant fob watch and was intended to be driven by the speedometer cable. It was a form of navigational aid, and came with a set of circular cards divided into a hundred equal spaces, each one representing one mile. On each disc was printed a route, and the disc revolved as the vehicle progressed and a pointer indicated printed directions at given mileages to enable the motorist to find his way from city to city. Since signposts were rare in rural America, and there was no national road network, it was obviously felt that there was a demand for the Live-Map-Meter, an example of which was discovered in Philadelphia in the 1960s.

Postage stamps

Postage stamps depicting cars are common—the first was issued by the United States in 1901—but most are of little value or interest to the historian, except as curios. However, in 1930 *The Autocar* announced that it would be issuing a set of 'stamps' depicting famous racing drivers. Compiled by its sports editor, Sammy Davis (who wrote under the *nom de plume* Casque) the stamps were actually labels prepared by stamp printers, the same size as ordinary postage stamps, and perforated in the same way. Printed in blue, they sold at 2s 6d a sheet of about 140 portraits of different racing drivers. The proceeds of the sale of the stamps was to be used to buy a trophy, to be known as the *Autocar Readers' Award*, to be presented to the mechanic of the winning car in the RAC Tourist Trophy Race in Ulster. Any surplus money would be handed over to the Weybridge Hospital, the local hospital for the Brooklands track, in which, by a sad irony, Sammy Davis was to be confined for some long time the following year after a serious crash in his Invicta during the Double Twelve race, when he hit a wire supporting a trackside telegraph pole. While Davis was still confined to hospital with a broken thigh, the staff of *The Autocar* presented him with a bronze statuette by Gordon Crosby depicting a racing car at speed, and inscribed 'to Sammy from his colleagues, premier award in his greatest trial'.

Mascots

It is not clear exactly when the first car mascots appeared; they were certainly preceded by club badges such as those of the Automobile Club of Great Britain and Ireland (later the RAC) and of the Automobile Association and the Motor Union, which merged in 1908. However, such badges were as much an insurance against speed trapping (members would be saluted by the club's patrol scouts if the road ahead was clear, but no salute would be forthcoming if there was a police trap in operation) as they were a decoration for the car. Certainly by about 1908 motorists were in the habit of attaching lucky charms to the radiators of their cars in the form of plush teddy bears or similar decorations and mascots of varying degrees of artistic merit began to appear on the radiator caps of motor cars.

Some of the first commercially produced mascots were offered by S. Smith & Son of London, the famous instrument makers. Early subjects included Gobbo, the lucky mascot, a small imp which sat on the radiator cap and represented a good luck character akin to his contemporary Billiken. There were also the Lincoln Imp, which sat on the radiator cap with one leg hanging down in front. But Smith's most expensive mascot of the time was the Flying Mascot, which represented a Gnome rotary aeroengine and propellor which rotated as the car went along. In aluminium the Flying Mascot cost £1 5s (£1.25), while in brass it was £1 7s 6d (£1.37½), three times as much as Gobbo.

The first car mascot to achieve true distinction was the famous Spirit of Ecstasy, offered from about 1910 by Rolls-Royce Limited in order to discourage Rolls-Royce owners from fitting unsuitable mascots to their cars. The Spirit of Ecstasy was designed by the sculptor Charles Sykes, and apparently modelled by Miss Ellen Thornton, secretary of the first Lord Montagu of Beaulieu, who was drowned with Lord Kitchener when the *Persia* was torpedoed off the Dardanelles in 1915.

Other companies followed suit with mascots specifically designed for one make of car; Peugeot offered a lion based on their trademark, the work of the sculptor Marx, while Vulcan of Southport, England, brought out a statuette of the blacksmith god Vulcan holding a steering wheel. In later years, the Belgian Minerva company crowned the radiator caps of their cars with a head of the Goddess Minerva, Pierce Arrow introduced the famous archer mascot, Amilcar capped their radiators with a statue of the flying horse Pegasus, and Peerless of America commissioned the famous Belgian sculptor de Soëte to create a stylised eagle for their radiator. Bazin, who had designed the original Amilcar Pegasus, also designed the famous flying stork mascot for Hispano-Suiza. And after the Great War, Renault commemorated the achievements of their light tanks by issuing a radiator mascot designed by Fix Marsseau, depicting a Renault FT 17 light tank climbing over an obstacle.

Though most manufacturers who fitted mascots did so willingly, Gebriel Voisin designed his mascot as a sop to fashion. The Voisin mascot, inspired by the work of Marcelle Lejeune, was a highly stylised bird formed from rivetted aluminium sheets; Voisin signified his contempt for his mascot by calling it 'La Cocotte', which apart from meaning 'birdie' in French is also used to describe a woman of easy virtue . . ..

In 1924, shortly after the Ford Company had taken over Lincoln, there was a world-wide contest among Ford companies to suggest a suitable subject for a radiator mascot. The competition was won by the Dutch Ford Company, which suggested a greyhound. The leaping greyhound mascot was subsequently used on Lincoln cars, and also used as an accessory on early Ford V8s. It appears to have been the inspiration for the original Jaguar mascot designed by the artist F. Gordon Crosby in the mid-1930s. Another piece of animal symbolism was the hare adopted as a mascot by Alvis cars, signifying that the Alvis car was 'always ahead of the pack'. Rover, on the other hand, used a Viking's head. They also adopted a Viking longship as their radiator badge which survives in almost unrecognisably stylised form on the latest Rover cars. One of the more unusual mascots of the 1920s was the Ole Bill head designed by the cartoonist

Modelled on the personal insignia of First World War flying ace, Georges Guynemer, the Hispano Stork was sculpted by F. Bazin. This particular mascot is mounted on a cap inscribed to the effect that the car to which it was fitted, a 37.2 hp Hispano-Suiza, lapped Brooklands at 88 mph at the Easter Meeting, 1922 (Foulkes-Halbard Collection).

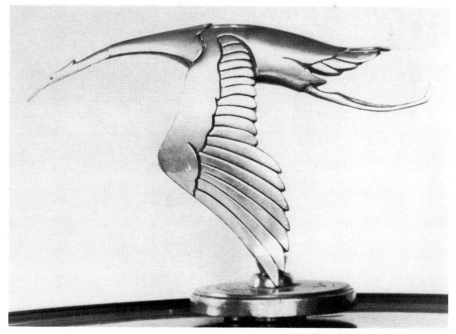

Bruce Bairnsfather, and depicting his famous First World War character remembered for his famous catch phrase 'If you knows a better 'ole go to it!'

Other mascots were distinguished as pieces of sculpture in their own right. Perhaps the supreme example was the Bugatti elephant, fixed only to the seven Bugatti Royale models ever built, and based on a metal seal handle designed by Rembrandt Bugatti, a talented young sculptor who committed suicide shortly after the outbreak of the Great War. Rembrandt Bugatti, perhaps the most gifted of the *Animalier* sculptors, had designed the seal for his brother who adapted it as a radiator mascot. In recent years a limited edition of reproductions of the Bugatti elephant has been brought out under the auspices of the Bugatti Owners Club. Among the other sculptors who created special radiator mascots were Leverrier, among whose work was a female dancer and a stylised eagle, and Luppi, whose radiator mascot *Le Bolide* was the winged head of a woman. Laplagne designed a kneeling Indian, Povlievrad created a man with an arrow, and many other 'one-off' mascots survive.

René Lalique was one of the most celebrated jewellers of the Art Nouveau period, and lived from 1860 to 1945. He offered a wide range of moulded crystal

Left *The Lalique 'Chanteclair' crystal car mascot is still being produced, though today it is sold as a paperweight. This, however, is a genuine Chanteclair of the late 1920s* (Foulkes-Halbard Collection).

Right *During the 1920s, France used to hold an annual* Concours du bouchon de radiateur. *This whimsical 'Elephant's Egg' was one of the winning mascots.* (Foulkes-Halbard Collection).

glass mascots, perhaps the most celebrated of which was Victoire, a female head with the mouth open and the hair streaming behind like a stylised headdress; this mascot is also known as Spirit of the Wind. Among his other offerings were a female nude, representations of cockerels and peacocks' heads, medallions and archers, a ram's head, a haughty eagle's head and 'Longchamps', representing a horse's head.

In 1966, a New York company, Jacques Jugeat Inc, announced that they were supplying new Lalique radiator mascots, presumably using moulds taken from the originals. It is difficult to see how one could tell such a reproduction from an original. And Lalique's beautiful glass mascots can command very high prices nowadays, as the fragile material from which they were made has not been conducive to a high survival rate. Some Lalique mascots had an electric light in their base so that they could be illuminated at night. Similar mascots, though not of such artistic merit, were offered by the Red-Ashay Company, and these could be had with a device which altered the colour of the electric light depending on the speed of the car. The Red-Ashay motor mascots were manufactured by H.G. Ascher Limited, of Chorlton on Medlock, Manchester. The colour changing was effected by a revolving propellor in the base of the mascot; other models offered 'four colours or combinations at the turn of a knob', and were said to be 'the *only* colour changing mascots'. Prices of the Red-Ashay mascots ranged from one guinea to ten guineas.

Other novelty mascots offered during the 1920s were the 'Kwiksail', a model aeroplane which arose on a vertical rod passing through the radiator cap as the speed of the car increased. Then there was the Movie Mascot, a model policeman pivoted on the radiator cap in such a way that it moved from side to side and waved its arms as the car braked, accelerated and turned. Other examples of humour in mascots included a couple of rare early caricature mascots by the celebrated poster artist, John Hassall. One of these depicted a moon faced aviator, whose features were made of ceramic material, seated in a little brass monoplane. Another mascot designed by Hassall was the 'Robert', sold by S. Smith & Sons of London, the celebrated motor accessory manufacturers, at 42 shillings in 1925. Described as 'an amusing design', the 'Robert' was a comic policeman with moveable head and helmet. Like the Hassall airman, it was made of brass with earthenware face and hands, with Hassall's signature engraved on it.

One of the most curious mascots ever offered appeared in 1926. This was the Trix sunshine mascot, also known as 'Spungie', which consisted of a head with protruding tongue, all made of sponge rubber, with a nickel plated clip to enable it to be fastened to the filler neck of a car. It was extremely hideous, and one doubts the claim made by its manufacturer, Eric J. Lever of Clerkenwell, that it 'sold on sight'. Then there was the Speed Devil, apparently originating in France, and intended to be fastened to the rear of sports cars to cock a snook at those who had just been overtaken.

In 1934, Desmo of Birmingham, one of the leading retailers of mascots, obtained permission from Walt Disney to model Mickey and Minnie Mouse as car mascots. These were not just made of plated metal, but were coloured to represent the originals and would have looked absolutely right on the radiator cap of an MG Midget or Singer Le Mans. One of the most curious mascots of the 1930s was offered in 1935 by Desmo. It was a miniature reproduction of a

Above left *This was the racing driver Luigi Villoresi's personal mascot. The work of E. Julliani, it depicts 'Gigi' Villoresi in his uniform as a Papal guard* (Foulkes-Halbard Collection).

Above *This bulldog with goggles was the mascot of the pioneer motor accessory company, the East London Rubber Company* (Foulkes-Halbard Collection).

Left *In 1907, the motoring monarch, Edward VII, bestowed royal patronage on the Automobile Club of Great Britain & Ireland; this was the King's personal silver RAC badge. Hallmarked 1907, it must have been one of the first club badges to be designed as a mascot* (Foulkes-Halbard Collection).

BBC microphone, and was a copy of a special presentation mascot designed for the radio comedian Leonard Henry. The mike mascot sold for 25 shillings (£1.25) and was chromium plated.

Perhaps the rarest mascots of all were those designed specifically for the cars of a famous personality of the day. Rudolph Valentino, for example, adorned his Voisin and Isotta Fraschini cars with a cobra mascot, to commemorate his role in the film of that name, while Jackie Coogan, who as a boy had starred with Charlie Chaplin in the film *The Kid*, had a brass and ivory model of himself in that role specially made for the radiator cap of his car.

And then, of course, there were the royal mascots, statues of Britannia and George and the Dragon created for the British Royal Family—the statue of George and the Dragon had to be especially designed for maximum strength, as it was found that the original conception had too thin a mass of metal connecting the upper part of the sculpture with the radiator cap and was therefore liable to metal fatigue. Other royal mascots included a statue of Britannia standing on top of the world with a lion at her side, and Britannia, her cloak streaming behind her, holding out an orb. Incidentally, all of George V's cars were fitted with two clocks in the rear compartment; one was a fixture, the other was a present to the King which was transferred from car to car.

In the early 1930s it was recommended that mascots protruding beyond the front of the car should not be fitted because they represented a danger to pedestrians in the event of a collision. This recommendation became law in 1937. In May 1932, the Birmingham Mascot Company brought out a flying stork mascot in which both the neck and beak of the bird were made of rubber, while the wings of the bird had alternate feathers tinted to match the colour of the rubber. And, of course, the snipe mascot fitted to the Humber Snipes of the 1930s had a rubber beak, which perished and fell out in old age, leaving an empty socket . . ..

Cigarette cards

The best-known sets of motoring cigarette cards are the two series of *Motor Cars* issued by Players in the 1930s, but the very first cards to depict cars were issued just after the turn of the century by Ogden's 'Guinea Gold' Cigarettes, and depicted such rarities as the Bertrand Motor Carriage. Lambert and Butlers issued several sets of cards, the second and third series of the 1920s being especially desirable. These featured Cubitt, Hispano-Suiza, Model T Ford, Lanchester 40 and other models of the day. The same firm brought out a series of motor cars in 1935, too, with illustrations of cars such as the Essex Terraplane (with English coachwork), Humber 12, BSA 10 hp and Jowett Kestrel.

Cars featured in a 1914-18 set, *Military Motors*, issued by Wills, showed such vehicles as 'King Victor's Car' and 'Anti-Aircraft Gun Motor'. Series which included illustrations of cars were Ogden's *Motor Races 1941*, which featured Alfa Romeo, Bugatti and Maserati cars, and *Speed*, a Wills set which showed Raymond Mays' ERA, Ab Jenkins' *Mormon Meteor*, John Cobb's Napier Railton and the Grand Prix Mercedes and Auto Union cars among examples of speed on land, sea and air. In recent years Brooke Bond Tea have issued a 'History of the Motor Car' in card form, with commentary by Peter Hull, Secretary of the Vintage Sports Car Club.

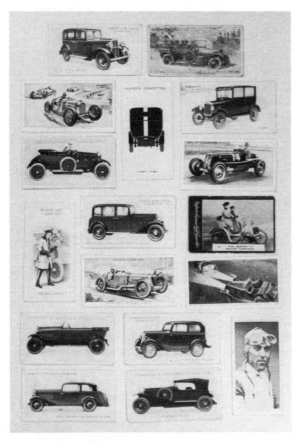

Motoring games

Among the games produced in the early days of motoring were *Toof Toof*, the motor car game and a similar game played with a teetotum and cards entitled *Tut Tut*: 'A run in a motor car, a new and exciting game'. It had cards showing a circa 1905 touring car and whose direction included '28 days in prison lose 20 points', 'summons lose 10 points', 'a police trap lose 5 points' and 'a puncture lose 2 points'. *Toof Toof* on the other hand had playing pieces in the shape of flat moulded lead motor cars: a whistle played a major part in the game.

Around 1903 a game called *Course d'Automobile* appeared in France: its lively cover depicted a motor race with a Paris-Madrid-like Mors racer thundering over the finishing line. Another early game was *Motor Tour*, issued in a number of forms over the years, in which competitors threw a dice to move from London to Edinburgh round a penalty-filled oval of 101 spaces, '101' being 'Over a precipice. Killed. Out of game'.

The Autocar's Sports Editor, Sammy Davis, devised a Brooklands race game for the toy-makers Chad Valley, sold in a box with a Gordon Crosby painting on the lid of Eyston's Panhard and Birkin's Blower Bentley in the 1932 Empire Trophy Race. The board showed the Brooklands circuit, the pieces were modelled on Bugattis, and the rules were a facsimile of the genuine Brooklands rule book.

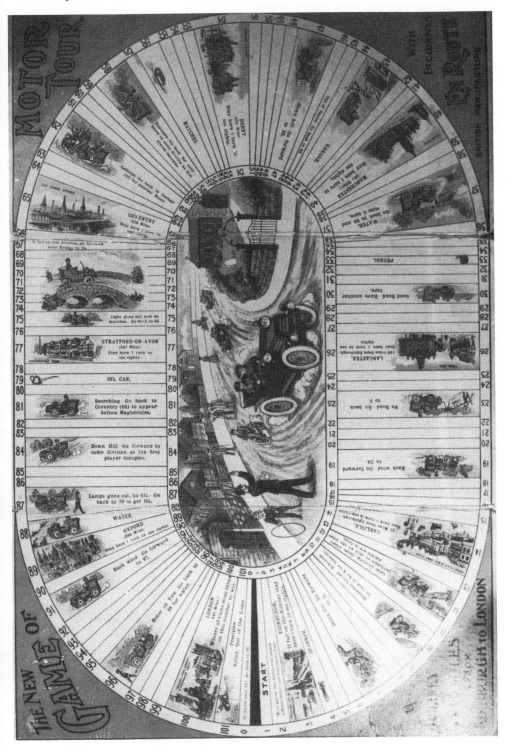

Left and below left *The box and some of the playing pieces for the game of 'Toof-Toof', dating from circa 1900. The whistle doubtless represents the police traps which were set to trap speeding motorists exceeding the open road limit of 12 mph (20 km/h) (Foulkes-Halbard Collection).*

Below *Dating from circa 1905, this German clockwork car appears to be based on a contemporary Cadillac design (Foulkes-Halbard Collection).*

Toys

Though the first crude toy motor cars appeared in the 1890s, it was in the early 1900s that the first popular—and accurate—models appeared. These ranged from 'penny toys' produced in France to elaborate clockwork models. In the 1920s, makers like the German firm Bing of Nuremberg produced pressed-steel cars in huge numbers, and French makers turned out truly beautiful scale model clockwork cars, some especially fine examples being produced by Citroën. Most sought-after of the clockwork toys of the interwar period is the P2 Alfa Romeo, issued in four series in the late 1920s.

Diecast toys were an innovation of the 1930s, superseding the crude cast-iron models of the 1920s. Dinky Toys in Britain and Tootsietoys in the US were the style leaders, though the metal they were made from can suffer distressing decay in old age. Also in the 1920s, pedal cars were made in replicas of full-size prototypes, even of Sir Malcolm Campbell's 350 hp Sunbeam racer. A pioneer in this respect was Tri-Ang; I met its founder, Walter Lines, around 1970 (he was then in his 80s) and he told me that he still kept the first pedal car he had built, in 1910, at his home in Godstone, Surrey.

Enamelled signs

Enamelled signs made their appearance in late Victorian days. They were especially suited to outdoor display, as vitreous enamel colours had a smooth surface which retained its brilliance far longer than either paint or printed posters and the metal backing, protected from rust by the enamel, was virtually indestructable. Very early on, the motor trade realised that enamelled signs were well suited to display on their premises, and the oil and petrol companies were among the first to produce signs aimed at the motorist. For example, the Moebius Challenge oil company produced enamel signs for motor dealers around 1898, and the red, black and yellow Pratts Perfection Spirit signs were a familiar feature of motor agencies in the early years of the 20th century.

Enamelled signs often survived far longer than the products they advertised; when their days of usefulness as an advertising medium were past, they were

A British Ford dealership circa 1926; the winged orange triangular enamelled sign on the wall was Ford's 'corporate sign' before the Great War.

often used for patching roofs or blocking holes in fences. Indeed, only a few years back, an entire shed made of period enamelled signs existed in a field in eastern Essex. Most motor manufacturers produced enamelled signs promoting their wares, and some of these can still be seen affixed to walls in rural areas. Among the best known enamelled signs were the blue and white roundels of Morris, and the winged orange triangle advertising the Model T Ford. However, in 1980 an earlier Ford enamel sign came to light in a garden in Southern England; about 18 inches across, it advertised the 15 hp Model N Ford and the 40/50 hp Model K six-cylinder, the only six-cylinder offered by the Ford Motor Company during the lifetime of Henry Ford. 'What is the use', demanded old Henry, smarting under the losses incurred by the poor-selling Model K, 'of a car that has more spark plugs than a cow has teats?'

Enamelled signs only began to fade from the scene with the coming of plastic billboards, which, while cheaper to produce, are far more fragile than the old signs. The nostalgia boom of the 1970s saw a number of replica enamel signs being produced, though the originals can still readily be found. Though many enamelled signs were simple in design (like the 'Union Jack' BP Petrol sign) others used the medium to maximum effect; a brightly coloured sign depicting a red car at speed and advertising 'British Dominion' tyres could be seen only a few years ago on the wall of an office building in Ilfracombe in Devon. Because they were often positioned in hard-of-access places, many enamel signs still survive in situ.

Most enamelled signs were single sided, to be nailed to a wall or fence, but there were some double-sided signs intended to project at right angles to a

Left *This delightful period Citroën bus stop sign marks where the workers of the Bugatti factory at Molsheim, Alsace, hailed the local bus on their way home.*

Right *An enamelled sign advertising Hispano-Suiza cars; rather a lordly marque, one might think, for such a publicity medium.*

building. One of the more unusual signs was that issued in the early 1920s which on one side advertised the GWK car, a friction-drive light car which had first appeared in 1911 (which had by the 1920s acquired a 10.8 hp Coventry-Climax engine mounted in the front instead of the two-cylinder Coventry-Simplex unit in the rear of the original). The other side advertised Bal-lon-ettes tyres. Intended for hanging in a motor agency, these signs were also to be seen screwed to the sides of the Bal-lon-ettes company's fleet of Model T Ford vans.

Innovations

Some innovatory ideas in car construction take a long time to become popular. In 1913 Henry Labourdette of Paris built the Prince Jacques limousine on a Rolls-Royce Silver Ghost chassis; the Prince Jacques design was remarkable in incorporating the first-ever sliding sunshine roof. It was not until 1926 that the sunshine roof idea was revived, in the shape of the Plein Ciel body, again by Labourdette, though this was a less elaborate device in which the car had a canvas roof which folded back over the rear seats. A similar design was offered by another Parisian coachbuilding company, Ansard and Teisseire.

Another idea which took many years to be generally adopted appeared in 1926—the 'universal horn switch' devised by a firm called Peasgood & Stanton of Holloway, North London. This was a lever fastened to the steering column which could be moved in any direction to sound the horn; it was the forerunner of today's indicator stalk control.

Some bright ideas were doomed to an early death, however. In 1932 an elderly mechanic from Pontiac, Michigan, named Erik Kjerp, contrived to produce a four-wheel-drive Model T Ford which also boasted four-wheel steering. The idea was that the car could move at an angle of 65 degrees, turn in its own length and slide in and out of parking places with ease. An eye witness commented, 'When this car goes through its weird movements, the manipulation seems to be accomplished by a maze of wheels, rods, levers and gears'. The battered state of the wings of the four-wheel-drive Model T show that even the optimistic Mr Kjerp had some difficulty in controlling the vehicle, and the idea proved short-lived.

On February 1 1933, Ferdinand M. Charles joined Morris Motors as a designer. Charles, born in France, but later becoming a naturalised British subject, graduated from the French school of art at the turn of the century and joined Rothschild. In 1902, Charles instigated the first ever fashion in motor bodywork by creating the famous Roi des Belges bodywork on a new Panhard for King Leopold of Belgium. Charles took his inspiration from the luxurious armchairs in the apartment of the King's *petite amie*, Cléo de Merode, and began a fashion which was to last the rest of the decade. In 1905, Charles joined the Daimler company and came to the public notice by his skill in design. Charles was also well ahead of his contemporaries in not merely drawing his body style, he made Plasticine mock-ups so that the customer could judge the outline of the car in three dimensions.

4 The People

Recording the past

The amazing thing about the motor car is that in the lifetime of many people still living, it has totally transformed society. But sadly, year by year the number of those who can recall the really early days of the motor car are growing fewer and fewer. Certainly there can be few people left alive who drove a car before the turn of the century. But there are still some nonagenerians who can remember what motoring was like in the first decade of the 1900s. Such men, I have found, often have amazingly retentive memories of events which took place 70 years ago. I have tape-recorded a number of them, and found that their recall of the past events often adds considerable interest to the bare facts of motoring history. I began recording such men on a big reel-to-reel recorder which has only the length of recording available on a large reel to commend it. Otherwise, it is clumsy and can inhibit the subject from speaking as freely as he otherwise might. The advent of the cassette recorder has made recording the memories of pioneer motorists a good deal easier. For a cassette recorder is small and inconspicuous, its microphone can be kept out of sight, and the cassettes themselves are easy to store and can readily be indexed by marking on the face of the cassette the space taken up by a particular interview.

One can still trace the pioneers of motoring through letters in the press, chance meetings, perhaps at an old car rally, or perhaps through an old people's home. Not all can be trusted for accuracy, but occasionally one does come across an interviewee whose memories are pure gold. For instance, some 15 years ago, I met an 85 year-old whose entire life had been spent as a mechanic. He had always played a humble role, yet by fortuitous chance he had often been present when motoring history was made. It was he, for instance, who had helped to build the very first Aston Martin car in 1914, using a 1.4-litre Coventry-Simplex engine in an Isotta-Fraschini voiturette chassis, and who had road-tested the first production Aston Martin in 1921. He had been the perfect 'fly on the wall' at many significant events, and had known personally many of the famous names of motoring history. Furthermore, he was blessed with almost total recall of events that had happened 70 years before.

Indeed, his memories went back to the late 1880s, when he had been red flag boy for the North Oxfordshire Steam Ploughing Company. He had first seen a motor car in the late 1890s, and had driven one soon after, helping his father in his cycle repair business, which in the way of the time, suddenly branched out into motor car repair, even though at that time there were no more than a few hundred horseless carriages in Britain. The interview, which illuminated many hitherto dark corners of motoring history, proved the indisputable necessity of priming oneself with the correct facts before undertaking such an interview. An interviewee is far more at his ease with someone who understands clearly what he is talking about, and can often be inspired to recall facts that he would otherwise have forgotten by an interviewer who is completely *au fait* with his subject.

In the mid-1960s, I interviewed some of the very few survivors of 19th century motoring; the youngest of them was in his late 80s and the oldest 103. Having thoroughly researched the topics on which I was going to interview them, I was able to refresh their memories of the names of people long dead, and places and events they had half forgotten. Once the memories had been unleashed, they tumbled out freely and illuminatingly.

Those of us who entered motoring journalism 20 years or more ago all knew St John Nixon well; Mr Nixon had taken part in the Thousand Miles Trial in 1900, when he was 14 years old and had become one of the most tireless motoring historians; he had also made a vast collection of early motoring literature, much of which survives in the library at the Veteran Car Club. I spoke to him on many occasions and he was always most illuminating and helpful with regard to the personalities whom he had known in the early 1900s; but when I interviewed one of his contemporaries, a man perhaps three or four years older than St John Nixon, he commented, with a delicious sense of inappropriateness 'You don't want to trust young St John's memory. He's not old enough to remember things properly!'

St John Nixon, however, told me how pioneer motor agent Charles Friswell had dropped dead after a game of tennis and how S.F. Edge had once chased a man who had pelted him with ice while he was motoring through Sussex around 1902 on a freezing cold night, caught him, compelled him to remove most of his clothing, and left it at the next village!

Motoring fashions

The first cars were totally devoid of weather protection, in which respect they paralleled their horsedrawn predecessors. So the clothes which had been worn

By the early 1920s, weather protection, even on open cars, had progressed to the state where no special motoring clothing was necessary, though the absence of heaters made thick coats vital for winter motoring.

when riding in a horsecarriage sufficed, so long as speeds remained low. Once cars began to be capable of real performance, the wind and dust became a real nuisance, and clothes designed specifically for motoring made their appearance. In Britain and America, dustproof overcoats were favoured; the light-coloured 'duster' coat symbolised the early motorists to the American public. But on the continent, the more sporting motorists affected aggressively shaggy fur coats, such as the *peau de bique* (goat's skin) and to keep the dust out, they adopted hideous face masks, some calculated to give observers nightmares of some motorised Inquisition.

Most lady motorists wore the fashionable mushroom-shaped hats, held down with a chiffon scarf; but high fashion also made its mark. One milliner showed a hat topped not with the fashionable stuffed birds, but with a tiny motorcar. The advent of tarred roads and weather protection in the form of windscreen and hood brought the end of motor fashions of this type. It was probably just as well, for the ugly motor clothes had only served to emphasise public antipathy towards the motorist.

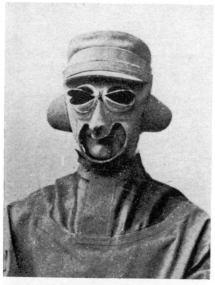 

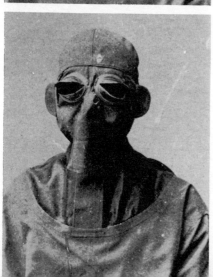 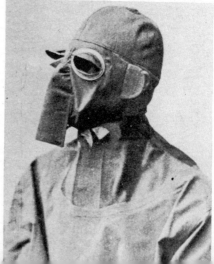

Left *These bizarre facemasks were devised in 1907 in Germany. Their curious design was intended to protect the wearer against flying dust from the untarred roads of the day.*

Above *Pioneer motorists had to dress up even for summer motoring, as this 1906 photograph of Fitzgerald Verity Dalton Esq and his family shows. Mr Dalton wears a linen dustcoat and a cap with veil to protect the back of his neck from the sun, and his family has wide-brimmed hats for the same reason. The canvas shield at the back of their 12 hp Darracq was to prevent dust from being sucked back into the tonneau.*

Driving licences

The first driving licence was issued on April 7 1891 to the engineer, Leon Serpollet, and his assistant, Averard, by the Commissioner of Police for Paris. It 'authorised them to drive either of the two steam carriages submitted to the examination of the Service des Mines on August 16 1889 and January 8 last, on all the roads of Paris'.

On August 14 1893 the Paris Police ordered that all motor vehicles should be operated with 'a regular authorisation issued by us on the demand of the owner. This authorisation can be cancelled by us at any time, at the instigation of the engineers'. Applicants had to pass a test of their competence to handle the vehicle. By the end of 1899 some 1,800 licences had been issued in the Paris region: from March 8 that year they had had to be produced on demand, and to carry a photograph of their bearer.

Though the first woman to drive a motor car had been Frau Berta Benz, who, with her two sons, took her husband's three-wheeled car on a circular tour from Mannheim, Germany, the first woman to pass a driving test was the Duchess d'Uzes, who, on May 21 1898, stepped aboard her 'automobile break' on a fine spring morning, accompanied by 'an engineer, specially sent by the Prefecture'. The Duchess, it was recorded, was 'wearing a fetchingly simple costume, with a little black felt hat tipped over one ear'. 'She took the tiller in her hand, manoeuvring it very expertly', and was duly awarded her licence.

Driving licences—unaccompanied by a test of skill, which it was felt was only applicable to 'motor servants'—were introduced into England by the Motor Car Act of August 14 1903, which came into effect the following New Year's Day. It set a minimum age limit of 17 for car drivers and 14 for motorcyclists. The driving test did not come into being until 1935.

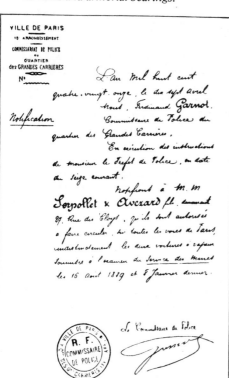

Above *As a cosmopolitan trading post, Shanghai was well ahead of the rest of China in entering the motoring age. This 'private motor car license No 33' was issued in September 1905, two years before the first car reached Peking.* **Below left** *The first driving licence issued in Paris, giving Léon Serpollet and his collaborator, Averard, permission to use steam carriages 'on all the roads of Paris'.* **Below right** *Discovered by the author in 1960, this unused licence application form for 1912 classes motorcars along with dogs, male servants and armorial bearings.*

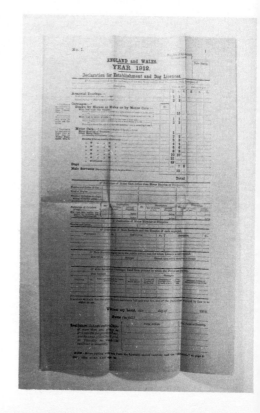

Museums Worldwide

Australia
Museum of Technology and Applied Arts and Science,
Sidney.

Austria
Technisches Museum für Industrie und Gewerbe,
Mariahilferstrasse 212,
Vienna.

Belgium
Collection Ghislain Mahy,
9000 Ghent.

Provinciaal Automuseum,
Kelchterhoef,
3530 Houthalen.

Channel Islands
Jersey Motor Museum,
St Peter's Village,
Jersey.

Czechoslovakia
Narodni Technicke Muzeum,
Kostelni 42,
Praha 7.

Denmark
Danmarks Tekniske Museum,
Ole Romers Vej,
Helsinge.

Aalholm Automobilmuseum,
Nysted.

France
Conservatoire National des Arts et Métiers,
292 rue St Martin
Paris 3.

Musée National de la Voiture et du Tourisme,
Château de Compiegne (Oise).

Musée Berliet,
Lyons.

Musée National de l'Automobile,
Château de Rochetaillée sur Saone (Rhône).

Musée de La Sarthe,
Le Mans (Sarthe).

Musée d'Automobiles de Normandie,
Clères.

Museon di Rodo,
Uzès (Gard).

Musée de l'Anthologie Automobile,
Saint Dizier (Haute Marne).

Musée Automobile de Provence,
Dellière Collection,
Route National 7,
Route de Cavillon,
13660 Orgon.

Musée de l'Aublette-en-Quevert,
Collection Edouard Bitel,
Route de St-Brieuc,
near Dinan.

Musée de Château de Fenelon,
Saint-Julien-de-Lampon,
24370 Carlux.

Collection Peugeot,
Usine Peugeot,
Sochaux-Montbeliard.

Musée de l'Abbatiale,
Collection Chassaing de Borredon,
Le Bec-Hellouin,
27800 Brionne.

Musée de Gerier,
Collection Serge Pozzoli,
27240 Buis-sur-Damville.

Musée Bonnal-Renaulac,
Collection Pierre Bonnal,
8 rue Ferdinand-Buisson,
33130 Begles-Bordeaux.

Musée Automobile de Bretagne,
Collection Desbordes,
Route de Fougeres,
35510 Cesson-Sevigne.

Musée Automobile du Forez,
Collection Lefranc,
Route D105,
42450 Sury-le-Comtal.

Musée Automobile du Val-de-Loire,
Route Nationale 7 Sud,
45250 Briare.

Musée de Lys-Chantilly,
Collection Rene Berte,
Rond-Point de la Reine,
60260 Lamorlaye.

Musée Automobile de Basse-Normandie,
Collection M Dubeck,
Place St-Juan,
61100 Flers.

Musée Schlumpf (Musée des Travailleurs),
Avenue de Colmar,
68000 Mulhouse.

Germany

Deutsches Museum von Meisterwerken
der Naturwissenschaft und Technik,
Museumsinsel 1,
Munich 8000.

Daimler Benz A.G. Museum,
Stuttgart Unterturkheim.

Japan

National Science Museum,
Kokuritu Kagaku Hakubutukan,
Ueno Park,
Tokyo.

Italy

Museo Storico Alfa Romeo,
Arese (Milan).

Centro Storico Fiat,
Via Chiabrera 20,
Torino.

Museo Vincenzo Lancia,
Via S Paolo 140,
Torino.

Museo Storico della Motorizzazione
Militare,
Cecchignola (Rome).

Museo Nazionale della Scienza e della
Tecnica,
Leonardo da Vinci,
Via San Vittore 21,
Milan.

Netherlands

Het Nationaal Automobilemuseum,
Veursestraatweg 280,
Leidschendam.

Norway

Norsk Teknisk Museum,
Fyrstikkalleen 1,
Etterstad, Oslo.

Portugal

Museu do Automovel,
Caramulo.

Museu Nacional dos Coches,
Lisbon.

Sweden

Tekniska Museet,
Museivägen 6,
Stockholm.

Skokloster Motor Museum,
Skokloster,
Mälären Sjö,
(Stockholm).

Switzerland

Maison Suisse des Transports et
Communications,
Lidostrasse 5,
Lucerne.

Musée de l'Automobile,
Château de Grandson,
Lac de Neuchatel.

Great Britain

Science Museum,
South Kensington,
London SW7.

National Motor Museum,
Beaulieu, Hampshire.

Herbert Art Gallery and Museum,
Cow Lane, Coventry,
Warwickshire.

Museum of Science and Industry,
Newhall Street,
Birmingham 3.

Art Gallery and Museum,
Kelvingrove,
Glasgow G3.

Transport Museum,
36 High Street,
Hull, Yorks.

City Museum,
Queens Road,
Bristol 8.

Stratford Motor Museum,
1 Shakespeare Street,
Stratford-upon-Avon.

Totnes Motor Museum,
The Quay,
Totnes, Devon.

Donington Collection,
Donington Park,
Castle Donington,
Derby DE7 5RP.

Bourton Motor Museum,
Bourton-on-the-Water,
Gloucestershire.

Caister Castle Motor Museum,
Caister-On-Sea,

Great Yarmouth, Norfolk.

Doune Motor Museum,
Doune, Perthshire.

USA

United States National Museum,
Smithsonian Institution,
Arts and Industries Building,
Washington 25 DC.

The Museum of Science and Industry,
Jackson Park,
Chicago 37,
Illinois.

Indianapolis Motor Speedway Museum,
4790 West 16th Street,
Indianapolis, Indiana.

Henry Ford Museum,
Greenfield Village,
Dearborn, Michigan.

Long Island Automotive Museum,
Museum Square,
Southampton 11,
New York.

Auburn-Cord-Duesenberg Museum,
Auburn,
Indiana.

Index